TAPESTRIES

TAPESTRIES

WORDS OF DEVOTION FOR
THE SECOND HALF OF LIFE

GAIL MESPLAY

SMYTH&HELWYS
PUBLISHING, INCORPORATED · MACON, GEORGIA

Smyth & Helwys Publishing, Inc.
6316 Peake Road
Macon, Georgia 31210-3960
1-800-747-3016
©2004 by Smyth & Helwys Publishing

Library of Congress Cataloging-in-Publication Data

Mesplay, Gail G.
Tapestries : words of devotion for the second half of life
by Gail G. Mesplay.
p. cm.
ISBN 978-1-57312-400-3
1. Meditations.
2. Aged–Prayer-books and devotions-English.
I. Title.
BL625.4.M47 2004
242'.65–dc22

2004006580

The power in a quote is sometimes
like the power in a seed.
—Sr. Lynne Elwinger, O.C.D.

CONTENTS

O

P

Q

R

S

T

V

W

TAPESTRIES

PREFACE

We did not weave the web of life. We are but a strand in it.

—Chief Seattle

For decades each of us has been the creator of a rich and colorful weaving: the tapestry of our lives. When someone begins a weaving, the first step is to warp the loom. The warp threads are the vertical stationary fibers that give the weaving its enduring foundation. In our lives, these threads are our families, communities, values handed down to us, and beliefs about life and death. After warping the loom, it is time to weave with colorful, pliant weft threads. These threads are the people we have encountered and loved and the experiences that have brought us joy, sorrow, and growth. There is no limit to the creativity manifested in the patterns we weave from these life events. Tapestries are long-lasting pieces of art, and even though they may wear thin in places or contain a few flaws, that only adds to their richness and enduring beauty. Some of the greatest weavers in the world are the Navajos. When they finish weaving a blanket or a rug, which is framed by a solid color, they carefully weave one thread of a different color through this frame. The thread is called a "spirit line," and it creates a path of escape for any part of the weaver's spirit that may have been caught inside the weaving. What a wonderful metaphor for finishing our life's tapestry.

The two hundred meditations in this dictionary-style book are written for those weaving their way through the second half of life. Choose among topics that speak to you in the moment or read through the book cover-to-cover as a daily devotional guide. I hope you will find helpful threads that can make your weaving brighter and more beautiful with each passing day.

AGE BEFORE BEAUTY

The golden age is before us, not behind us.

—St. Simon

As young people, we were taught always to be polite to the elderly. Now we are the ones who are frequently asked if we would like our groceries taken to the car or if we would like our shopping bags packed lightly. We should be pleased with such courtesy, but often we wonder, "Do I really look like I am incapable of doing this for myself?" Getting older sneaks up on us. One day we are treated like robust and vigorous people, and then in what seems to be in a twinkling of an eye, younger people give us unsolicited assistance and condescending looks. "Age before beauty" somehow implies that if you have the first, you can't have the second. Maybe the best approach to those who seem condescending is to take advantage of their kindness and consider it a perk that our age and our beauty rightfully deserve.

Age like distance adds a double charm.

—Oliver Wendell Holmes

ALONENESS

We are all aware of how many lonely people there are in our world. They are not only the homeless who have no warm place to sleep or the old people living in nursing homes. The lonely surround us every day, and we can often tell who they are by looking into their eyes. We all have lonely moments when we wish there was someone around. When we are by ourselves and feel the darkness of loneliness around us, it is hard to see ourselves as part of something bigger than our own daily lives. Albert Einstein called this common feeling of separation "a kind of optical delusion of consciousness." He felt this delusion created a prison and that our major task was to escape from it. If we give up our isolating thinking and our isolated ways, we will be able see that we are a part of a whole and are eternally linked together. Allowing our compassion to reach out to all living creatures can help the loneliness abate, for then we can feel a connection with all the facets of our world.

ALTARS

The most beautiful thing we can experience is the mysterious.

—Albert Einstein

When we enter many homes throughout the world, the first thing we encounter is the family altar. In Japan we see the family ancestors being honored; in India and Nepal we see images of Shiva, Krishna, Kali, or other Hindu deities. In Buddhist homes there may be a beautiful painting of the Lord Buddha lit by butter lamps, and in Roman Catholic homes, throughout the world, the altar may hold a statue of the Virgin Mary surrounded by candles that burn all through the day and night. The altar is the heart of these homes, and its beat resonates throughout the house. In homes where religion might not be the major focus of a family's daily life, we still see altars, but of a different nature. They may be on a bookshelf where pictures of the family or a collection of family treasures are displayed. Creating altars, whether of a secular or a religious nature, allows us to create a space that is distinct and different from the rest of our home. These altars can remove us from our mundane thoughts and actions and take our spirits to a place where we feel loved, protected, and comforted.

An altar is a shield, stronger than a fortress.

—Aeschylus

AMNESTY

Forgiveness is the attribute of the strong.

—Gandhi

To grant amnesty means to pardon someone or offer them forgiveness. Amnesty comes from the Greek word *amnestia,* which means oblivion. Often we carry around resentments and grudges for such a long time that we may forget the offense, but we continue to nurture the emotion. Not being able to forgive another can keep a wound from healing. In fact, it allows the injury to fester. Saying "I forgive you" releases our hearts from a prison that has the strongest bars. Our souls cannot afford to be enclosed in a space called "unforgiveness." To whom do you need to grant amnesty?

Write the wrongs that are done to you in the sand but write the good things that happen to you on a piece of marble.

—Arabic Proverb (adapted by VanEkeren)

ARROGANCE

Every man will fall who though born a man, proudly presumes to be a superman.

—Sophocles

The ancient Greeks used the word *hubris* to mean a lack of self-knowledge, excessive pride, arrogance, and presumptuousness. They believed it was a universal failing but would not go unpunished. The theme of *hubris* was developed in their theater and political philosophy. Perhaps the Greeks knew that for the first democracy in the world to succeed, *hubris* had to be held in check. Today we often blame the rich and famous for arrogance and excessiveness, but *hubris* can be found in each and every one of us. The Greeks believed the only antidote to this human failing was to lead a life of moderation and self-reflection—thus their famous principles of "Nothing to excess" and "Know thyself." When we feel self-absorbed and expect to get whatever we desire, we must remember that pride and arrogance do not bring success or allow for much humility or self-knowledge.

Everywhere man blames nature and fate, yet his fate is mostly but the echo of his character and passions, his mistakes and weaknesses.

—Democritus

AWARDS

The human heart is made for universal praise.
—Brother David Steindl-Rast

Throughout our lives we receive many awards: perfect attendance, citizenship, scouting, athletic, and academic. It is fun to go back through our lives, picturing what the award actually looked like and how we felt when we accepted it. It is often easier, however, to remember the awards we wanted to win but another received. It is unfortunate that our disappointments are often more vivid memories than our successes. What is an award you would like to receive at this moment in your life? What are your achievements and what are you working hard to do? Would you like to receive a Good Samaritan, a Friend to the Environment, or maybe a Nurturing of Neighbors Award? Even though it is wonderful to receive recognition, it is often enough to know we have tried our hardest to do our best and that this hard work has allowed us to deeply touch the lives of others.

Maybe one these days I'll be able to give myself a gold star for being ordinary and maybe one of these days I'll give myself a gold star for being extraordinary— for persisting. And maybe one day I won't need to have a star at all.

—Sue Bender

BEST FRIENDS

To me faire friend you never can be old,
For as you were when first your eye I eyde,
Such seemes your beautie still.

—William Shakespeare

Best friends change as we move through different phases and periods of our lives. Try making a list of the special people who have made you the person you are today. When you complete your list, think carefully about each of these good friends. What were their favorite things to do? What did their voices sound like? What color were their eyes? What is one of the happiest moments you can remember sharing with them? When you have time, write a letter to one of these distant friends, telling them what you are most grateful for in your relationship with them. Send this letter with the hope that your thoughts will deepen and energize the friendship even more.

If we discovered that we had five minutes left to say all
that we wanted to say, every telephone booth would be
occupied by people calling other people to stammer that
they loved them.

—Christopher Morley

BIRTHDAYS

To be 70 years young is sometimes more cheerful and hopeful than to be 40 years old.

—Oliver Wendell Holmes Jr.

Do you remember the birthday when it was announced that a second box of candles had to be purchased because on your last birthday your cake needed the entire box? You probably thought that day would never come. Now you might be anticipating the announcement that a third, fourth, or even fifth box will be needed. Birthdays seem to roll around faster and faster, and moving from one decade to another seems more like moving from one year to the next. Often as years fly by we begin to dread approaching birthdays, but if we see them as beginnings rather than markers of passing time, we might be able to truly enjoy them. Seeing a birthday as a start of a new year and new adventures can help make the event a valuable one. What resolutions could you make on your next birthday that would change your attitude toward aging?

The longer I live, the more beautiful life becomes.

—Frank Lloyd Wright

BLACK HOLES

The universe is wider than our view of it.
—Henry David Thoreau

Six thousand years ago, our ancestors struggled to find explanations for the natural but terrifying events that occurred in their lives: total eclipses of the sun, volcanic eruptions, and winds with hurricane force. Because they had no scientific way to explain these catastrophic events, they turned to their deities for explanations. In modern times, when we are faced with one of nature's mysteries we turn to our meteorologists, geologists, and astronomers. Sometimes, however, we simply cannot understand their explanations of quasars, fractals, and quarks. So, like our early ancestors, we are left with potentially frightening unknowns. Black holes are one of these baffling mysteries, for we are told that a black hole can devour everything around it: planets, stars, and even galaxies. What would happen to us if we fell into a black hole? Experts think we might be simultaneously stretched and crushed as we are pulled into the center. They have coined a word to describe this phenomenon: *spaghettifacation*. Scientists can predict volcanic eruptions, droughts, and tornadoes, but they still leave us with concerns that give us a taste of what it would have been like to be a Neolithic man or woman. It is doubtful there will ever be a time that will be devoid of unknowns. Would we want to live in a world that did not contain some unsolved mysteries?

I feel such a sense of solidarity with all living things that it does not matter to me where one begins and ends.
—Albert Einstein

BYWAYS

The great thing in this world is not where we are going, but in what direction we are traveling.

—Oliver Wendell Holmes

Some of the major expressways and highways of Europe have been built over ancient Roman and medieval roads. When we hike into wilderness areas we are often walking the same worn paths that native peoples carved out as they hunted and gathered in the woods and plains of the Americas. All these highways and byways were laid across the land so people could connect with one another, find food, and make peace and war. We all have favorite roads and trails that we travel on—some simply for the trip and not the destination. What are your favorite roads, trails, and paths? Where do they take you? With whom do you travel? Is the destination or the traveling the most important part of your trips? What highways and byways do you still need to travel?

If a man wishes to be sure of the road he treads, he must close his eyes and walk in the dark.

—St. John of the Cross

CALENDARS

Time is a sort of river of passing events, and strong is its current; no sooner is a thing brought to sight than it is swept by and another takes its place, and this too will be swept away.

—Marcus Aurelius

Can you imagine a life without calendars? Many of us might rejoice, but they are the major way we organize and plan our days. We often take for granted our well-constructed twelve-months-a-year calendar and rarely think about how and why it came to be. Our calendar comes from the Romans and is based on the sun; other cultures have used the moon or even special stars, which caused serious timekeeping problems. An important timekeeping decision our ancestors had to make was where to start their calendar year. Most cultures picked a momentous event in their history and began counting from that point. The result is that people in different parts of the world live by different calendars and call months and years by different names and numbers. When our calendar starts controlling us and imposing a routine that we might not consciously choose, we must keep in mind that our ancestors created weeks and months only in order to keep track of major events such as when to plant and harvest and when to celebrate religious festivals. We must be grateful for this organizing tool, but we must not let it dictate the rhythm and order of our lives.

Time is nature's way of keeping everything from happening at once.

—graffiti, Dallas, Texas

CANDLES

Unshared joy is an unlighted candle.

—Spanish Proverb

The light of a candle is a blessing that sanctifies a moment. Touching a match to a candle wick moves us from our busy daily lives into a realm of celebration and mystery. When we light Hanukkah, Advent, or birthday candles, a call is made for the community to gather and witness a special event. Our world looks different in candlelight; objects and people take on a soft glow and edges disappear. When you want magic and mystery in your life, light a candle. When you feel a need to move from the mundane to the sacred, light a candle. When you want to blot out your daily concerns and recollect your thoughts, light a candle.

Forgetfulness in the darkness;
mindfulness in the light.
I bring awareness
To shine upon all life.

—Thich Nhat Hanh

CARING

Every time you hurt someone and then grieve inside because of it, you are attending a valuable seminar on sensitivity.

—Eknath Easwaran

It is easy to become so self-absorbed that we are unaware of other people's feelings or needs. We do not consciously choose to be insensitive, rude, or uncaring; we just get so caught up in our own problems and activities that we fail to recognize the needs of those around us. We know how hurtful this can be, for we have all had our feelings ignored. When we realize that we are dwelling more on ourselves than those around us, that is the time to change our self-centered focus and gently reach out to others.

Goodness is the only investment which never fails.

—Henry David Thoreau

CELEBRATIONS

I celebrate myself, I sing myself.

—Walt Whitman

Most of us mark on our calendar special days that we never let pass without having a party, sending a card, or making a phone call. For some of us, a year would not be complete without Hanukkah, Christmas, New Year's, Kwanzaa, or Thanksgiving celebrations. But why not have other days to celebrate? We all have dates we quietly remember every year: the birthday of a grandmother, the day when someone close to us passed away, the anniversary of the move into a home we have loved. These dates commemorate a special person or moment in our lives and deserve to be recognized. The celebration might be sitting quietly with photos or writing special people who shared this event with us. If we set this date aside and mark it for celebration, we will add a new holiday to our year.

We do not remember days, we remember moments.

—Anonymous

CEREMONY

Wake up. Wake up!
You have slept millions and millions of years.
Why not wake up this morning?

—Rumi

In many cultures of the world the first thing done each morning is a ceremony to greet the new day. The Hindu's morning ceremony, which is called *puja*, is to make an offering of water, flowers, fruit, and incense at a shrine or at the family altar. The Pueblo Indians of Arizona and New Mexico say "good morning" to the day by scattering cornmeal on the thresholds of their homes. Many Roman Catholics start their days by going to an early-morning mass. Most of us, however, have an entirely different morning ritual: we brush our teeth, fix coffee, feed the cat, retrieve the newspaper, and then rush about preparing for the day's activities. In the hustle and bustle of beginning a new day we often forget what a blessing it is to be given a fresh new start. What could we add to our morning routine that would make us stop for a while to think about what the new day means to us? What small gestures and words would make us pause and thank the universe for a new day?

If the only prayer you said for the rest of your life was
"thank you," that would suffice.

—Meister Eckhart

CHANGES

Even a thought, even a possibility can shatter us and transform us.

—Nietzsche

Arnold Toynbee dedicated a twelve-volume history of the world, *The Study of History*, to one question: Why did some of the greatest civilizations of all time fall? After dedicating forty years to this query, he concluded that civilizations fall because they refuse to change with the challenges of their time. Toynbee listed twenty-six great civilizations that met this fate because they were inflexible. His theory about cultures is also true for us as individuals. Most of us, as we grow older, hate to change the things we love—jobs, homes, and relationships. However, if we are inflexible, we will stagnate and become unhappy with our lives. When we are willing to accept the inevitability of change and respond creatively to it, we will be able to survive and thus not meet the fate of so many of the great civilizations of the world.

Progress is not an accident but a necessity. . . . It is part of nature.

—Herbert Spencer

CHATS

Talking with one another is loving one another.
　　　　　　　　　　　　　—Kenyan Proverb

Being with friends adds to a day. Catching up on each other's lives, families, and travel makes us feel connected. So often the conversation is light and might not have a lot of substance, but the purpose of our words is to weave a web of familiarity and caring. Words are a way to reach out and touch each other. Sometimes when we look for things to talk about, we thoughtlessly begin discussing other people. This can begin harmlessly, but we often embellish the story, make judgments, and turn the conversation into a gossip session. This can be dangerous not only to the party we're discussing but also to us, for it hurts our credibility and our trustworthiness. If chats turn to harmful gossip, we must do our best to steer them to another topic so that the hurtful words are stopped. We must ask ourselves whether we would want this conversation to be about us.

We must be as courteous to a man as we are to a picture,
which we are willing to give the advantage of good light.
　　　　　　　　　　　　　—Ralph Waldo Emerson

CHILDHOOD

Touching childhood memories can help open us up.
—Tulku Thondup

Exploring our childhood gives us an understanding of the person we are today. Find a picture of yourself when you were a young boy or girl. Take a close look. Do you remember when the picture was taken? How old were you? What were your favorite things to do at that age? Who were your friends? What did you like to do together? Where were your favorite places to play? What were your favorite toys and possessions? What did you enjoy doing with your family? What were your favorite books? What eight adjectives would describe you at that age? How many of these adjectives would others use to describe you today? What other similarities are there between the person in the photo and the person gazing at it? The young person looking back at you was totally unaware of all the experiences he/she would have. Is there anything you would like to tell this young you? What do you think this child would like to tell you?

Wisdom is like having a thousand eyes.
—Tibetan Proverb

CHIVALRY

Say something nice to someone else and watch the world light up with joy.

—Anonymous

One of the most sacred codes of conduct that existed in the Western world was the medieval knight's vow of chivalry. At the time of his knighthood the young nobleman promised to honor God and his lord, protect the old, the weak, and women, and to be brave under any situation. Adhering to this code brought order to the kingdom by establishing a standard of behavior. To break the code brought dishonor not only to the knight but also to his monarch. In today's world it appears that people make up their own individual codes of conduct. Unfortunately, what one might feel is correct behavior, another might consider improper. This leads to conflicts where both parties may become frustrated, rude, or even filled with rage. We see the absence of courtesy on our highways, at sporting events, and in shopping malls. We cannot change how others act, but we can change our responses to their behavior. Maybe if we meet a discourteous gesture with a courteous one or a frown with a smile, we can help the other person realize that our world is small, our time is short, and it is of utmost importance to be gentle and kind to one another.

. . . everything, absolutely everything counts.

—Sogyal Rinpoche

THE CIRCUS

When one stops wondering at the wonderful it stops being wonderful.

—Chinese Proverb

At least once in our lives, most of us have thought about escaping from the everyday routine to become a nomadic entertainer. If you could run away and join the circus, what would you most like to be? Some of your choices may be ring master, lion tamer, fireeater, trapeze artist, tightrope walker, or even a roustabout who puts up and takes down the giant circus tent. What a wonderful fantasy to imagine ourselves riding on the back of an enormous elephant or being the clown that brings smiles to everyone. Most of us cannot run away and join a circus, but in our imagination we all can become a part of its magic. We must make opportunities to enjoy events that "stuff our eyes with wonder," and we need to remember Albert Einstein believed that "imagination is more important than knowledge." When did you last go to a circus? You don't have to be a child or take a child to enter into the magic of the Big Top.

One's real life is often the life that one does not lead.

—Oscar Wilde

CLOCKS

Personal Electronics Inc., New York, has introduced a $100 watch with a "speak button." If the alarm is set, the watch plays a minuet at the appointed hour. If the wearer does nothing, five minutes later the watch will play a short piece, and a synthesized voice will announce "Please hurry."

—Wall Street Journal, 15 May 1981

How many times in a day do you check your clock or watch? "Time is money" and "time is scarce" are thoughts that float through our minds as we rush through life. Throughout history man has struggled to be precise in measuring hours and days. The ancient Sumerians came up with the sundial, and during the tenth century one could even carry around a pocket sundial. In the seventeenth century, pendulum clocks were invented. That was still not precise enough, so inventors worked away. In the 1930s and 1940s, timekeeping took a leap forward with the quartz crystal. A few years later, scientists completed the first cesium atomic beam device, and a clock was invented that keeps time to one-millionth of a second per year. Even better is the possibility of one that uses ultrarapid laser flashes. An "optical frequency" atomic clock would be 100,000 times more accurate than the current standard way of measuring time. Do we want to move through the second half of our lives counting not just minutes but fractions of seconds? Is this really the civilized way to live? Would you be willing to refuse to use a clock or watch for just one day? If you were brave enough to try this, how would your day be different?

I must govern the clock, not be governed by it.
—Golda Meir

COCOONS

Every moment nature starts on the longest journey and every moment she reaches her goal.

—Goethe

As children we loved to search the land for the tiny cocoons that hung from delicate stalks of weeds and twigs. When we discovered one of these tiny treasures, we would carefully snip off the stem and gently carry it home, place it in a clear glass jar, and watch its life unfold. If we were skillful nurturers, we were given the gift of seeing a tiny creature undergo metamorphosis. Even at a young age, we understood the meaning of this long word, for we witnessed the unseen caterpillar, encased in its self-created womb, slumber deeply and then emerge as one of the most beautiful creatures in nature. Nature does not have to be told about the importance of patience, for patience is its job. When we feel trapped within our bodies or our present circumstances, we need to remember that we were all given the ability to be patient and that all we need to do is be more caterpillar-like and relax into the next unknown stage of life.

We can become like silkworms trapped by their silk. We reach a state where we suffocate with our own views, feelings, habits, and reactions.

—Tulku Thondup

COINS

Histories make men wise.

—Francis Bacon

Have you ever held an ancient coin in the palm of your hand? Holding one is much like entering a time machine that can whisk us back through history. Ancient Roman coins survived the fall of one of the mightiest empires of the world, weathered the Middle Ages when they lost all their inherent worth, and then often lay buried until unearthed by a farmer's plough or the spade of an archaeologist. A coin can take you by the hand and lead you back on a time line through eras of war and times of peace, through depressions and prosperity, and through political turmoil and reconciliation. If this small artifact could talk, it would tell you of its travels across mountain ranges, through kingdoms, and through tiny villages and great cities. Coins have always fascinated people because by touching them we can touch countless other men and women who jingled them in their pockets and pouches, stored them in wooden chests and piggy banks, and even tossed them into a well or fountain for good luck. Try to find an old coin and let it take you on a journey through history and introduce you to sights that you have known only through the pages of history books.

The whole past is the procession of the future.

—Thomas Carlyle

COLLECTIONS

We are shaped and fashioned by what we love.

—Goethe

The variety of collections people have is staggering: stamps, coins, paintings, Barbie dolls, barbed wire, teacups, and even homes. People who live at a subsistence level do not have the luxury of being collectors. Having one coin, one book, or even one cup might be all they can afford. Their homes, which often house an extended family, do not have the space for collections of non-utilitarian items. Most collectors have plans to pass their treasures down to family members or friends, but this does not mean others will appreciate or value this inheritance. We must, therefore, enjoy these things while we can and not expect others to appreciate or care for them in the way we do. It would be interesting if we could begin to collect intangible things: acts of compassion, hours of service, kindly remarks, or minutes of patience. These are truly a legacy that will have a longer-lasting value than any object we have on our shelves and walls.

The only wealth which you will keep forever, is the wealth which you have given away.

—Martial

COLOR

The purest and most thoughtful minds are those who love color the most.

—John Ruskin

Can you imagine what it would be like to live in a black and white world? We would not have bluebirds, bluebells, or ruby-throated hummingbirds. We would have no way to describe the color of a sunset or the eyes of someone we love. We would not have words to describe our moods and emotions: feeling blue, green with envy, seeing red. So often we do not take the time to look at all the colors that surround us—the many shades of green found in just one tree or the different colors found in the fur of an animal we love. Colors hold memories. What was your favorite color as a child? What was the color of your favorite outfit, the color of your room? What is your favorite color now? It is fun to invent new names for all the colors we see in one day's time: mud cake brown, spider black, paraffin white, tomato soup red, English muffin beige. When we try to describe a color with words, we are forced to absorb it and give it our one-pointed attention.

Nothing reaches the intellect before making its appearance in the senses.

—Latin Proverb

COMPASS

Some individuals seem to have been born with a built-in compass. You can spin them around and around, and when they stop they can point due north. There are others who could not point west even while watching a sunset. Almost all people, however, possess an inner compass that helps them find the path between right and wrong. This compass is able to point them to an ethical North Pole, the direction that will guide them to right thinking and altruistic action. Sometimes the difference between right and wrong behavior is difficult to sort out. If we stop for a few minutes, however, and get our bearings from the compass located within our hearts, we will easily be able to see the arrow pointing us in the "right" direction.

I can't say I was ever lost, but I was bewildered for three days.

—Daniel Boone

CONNECTING

Ultimately, the entire universe . . . has to be understood as a single individual whole.

—David Bohm

In 1964, the physicist John S. Bell came up with one of the most startling discoveries in the history of science. Bell's Theorem proposed that a change in the spin of one particle in a two-particle system would immediately change its twin no matter how large the distance between them. The scientific community found this almost unthinkable. How could one particle know when its twin had changed? In order for this to happen the signal would have to be faster than the speed of light. Nevertheless, time and countless experiments have proven Bell's Theorem to be true. Simply put, when two particles meet, say "hello," and then are separated beyond the ends of the universe, if one changes the other will instantaneously change as well. For most of us this scientific information is hard to absorb, and yet if we apply it to personal relationships it makes all the sense in the world. We all have significant people in our lives to whom we feel so connected that no matter how much time or space comes between us, we can never truly be separated. The bond created between us will always be in existence, and we will always be able to resonate with each other.

All real living is meeting.

—Martin Buber

CONSCIENCE

Their consciences told them to save as many lives as they could, even if doing this meant endangering the lives of all the villagers, and they obeyed their consciences.
—Phillip Hallie, *Lest Innocent Blood Be Shed*

An amazing story of bravery that came out of World War II took place in a little mountain town in southern France by the name of Le Chambon. During the most horrific time of the war the citizens of this small village stood up against the insanity of fascism. Led by their Protestant pastor, Andre Trocme, they opened their village to hundreds of Jews, mostly children, and hid these refugees in their churches, schools, and homes. These French men and women were not fighting for the liberation of a country; they were fighting to save the lives of total strangers. To be caught meant death and also the possible destruction of the entire village. Most of us have not had to be tested in this way, but if you were, what do you think you would do? It is hard to know until the situation arises, but it is important to reflect on our beliefs and ethical code so we will be prepared, if necessary, to act on our conscience.

This I think is my kind of religion. You see, it is a way of handling myself.
—Magda Trocme, wife of Pastor Andre Trocme, Le Chambon

CONSERVATION

I am in love with this green earth.

—Charles Lamb

By the time we reach seventy years of age, we will have drunk 26,000,000 tons of water, consumed 28,000 pounds of milk and cream, used 21,000 gallons of gasoline, and eaten 9,000 pounds of wheat. In one year, Americans use up enough trees to build a 10-foot-wide walkway thirty times around the world at the equator. Our nation consumes half of the world's total resources, and yet we are only one-fifteenth of the population of the earth. There is not one of us who consciously chooses to be greedy, and yet our choices are robbing the earth and other humans of their fair share. By simplifying our lives we can begin to spread out the wealth, and by sharing we will discover that there are enough resources to satisfy the needs of everyone who lives upon this planet. What changes can you make in your lifestyle that will allow others to enjoy all of the necessities you take for granted?

To be content with little is difficult, to be content with much, impossible.

—Proverb

CONTROL

Most of us acknowledge the virtue of self-control, but to judge by our actions, what we would really like to control is others.

—Eknath Easwaran

When we find ourselves the victim of another person's controlling behavior, we often react with anger and indignation: "How dare this person think they can tell me what to do! "We all want to be in control of our lives, so when another imposes their will or agenda on us we are bound to react strongly to their attempt to manipulate. We must remember how we feel about being controlled when we attempt to control someone else. Most of us do not want to be a manipulator, but often our strong self-will pushes us into controlling behavior. We all want our own way, for we feel that this is a way to gain happiness. The best way to achieve peace, however, is to listen to the needs of others and not attempt to control them. Real joy comes from putting others first.

Evil deeds like perfume are hard to hide.

—African Proverb

COUNTING BLESSINGS

Gratitude is the heart's memory.

—French Proverb

For what are you most grateful? A wonderful time to think about these gifts is when you first open your eyes in the morning or as you prepare for bed at night. As you move through your day, it is important to say thank you to anyone or for anything that crosses your path and brings you delight, hope, and happiness: the rose outside your window, the garbage man taking away your trash, or even an afternoon moment when you can take a refreshing nap. Brother David Steindl-Rast, author of *Gratefulness, the Art of Prayer,* suggests that we should not depend on happiness to make us grateful but on gratitude to bring us happiness.

> *There is as much greatness in acknowledging a good turn as in doing it.*
>
> —Seneca

CROSSES

Gentle time will heal our sorrows.

—Sophocles

We see in increasing numbers small wooden crosses decorated with plastic flowers along our highways. These memorials mark the spot where someone has met a tragic death, and grieving loved ones have marked the place so all who pass by will know the tears shed at this location. These roadside shrines are called *descansos*, which in Spanish means "resting spot." It is from a tradition found in Spain where the place at which pallbearers rest is marked with crosses. This custom was brought to the New World and became an important part of the grieving process for the Spanish who immigrated to the American Southwest. Two centuries ago, hundreds of these wooded crosses stretched across this barren land, marking the places where settlers had died. Today the crosses tell us about the dangers of American highways and how in an instant a life can be taken from us. When you pass one of these crosses on the road, take a moment to think of the life that was lost at this place and vow to drive with care and love so that fewer *descansos* will be erected on the edges of our roads.

> *In the rising of the sun and in its going down, we remember them.*
>
> —Jewish Prayer

CYCLES

Silently sitting by the window
Leaves fall and flowers bloom.
The seasons come and go.
Could there be a better life?

—Zen Poem

What is your favorite season? What is your favorite hour of the day? Have you noticed that you feel more vitality during certain times of the year? All of nature goes through cycles: the moon waxes and wanes; summer ends and winter arrives; the sun rises, arches across the sky, and descends at dusk. These movements are bound to have an effect on our emotional and physical cycles. We all need to be aware of when we feel our best and use these peak times in our busy lives. There are seasons when we need to hibernate and times of the day when we need to retreat for a moment of solitude and rest. King Solomon gave us excellent advice: "To everything there is a season and a time to every purpose under heaven."

But if in your thoughts you must measure time into sea-
sons let each season encircle all the other seasons, and let
today embrace the past with remembrance and the future
with longing.

—Kahlil Gibran

DARK DAYS

Suffering and death are not enemies, but doors leading to
new levels of knowledge and of love.

—Fr. Thomas Keating

Even if the sun is shining brightly in a cloudless sky, we can have a
dark and gloomy day. Most of the time we are aware of what has made
the ominous interior dark clouds move in: stress at home or work, a
betrayal, a mistake we made, or separation from a loved one. Some
days, however, we cannot pinpoint the reason for the bleak feeling that
quickly descends and covers us with despair. During these times it is
hard to be encouraged when friends remind us of "silver linings" or
the "light at the end of the tunnel." All we want to do during these
times is retreat into the darkness. Growth sometimes simply needs
moist and silent soil to rest in for awhile.

Now, my loneliness
After the fireworks.
Look, a falling star.

—Anonymous

DARKNESS

Darkness can be a paradox. As we drive alone at night down a dark road, we often feel disoriented by the blackness and fearful about the unknown territory through which we travel. When we are tucked safely in our homes, however, the lengthening shadows of night make us feel peaceful, safe, and cozy. Outside and alone we feel vulnerable and insecure; inside our homes we feel protected and safe. It is tempting to stay in our nests and not take the risk to venture out. This can, however, become a habit and prevent us from having new and enriching adventures. Sometimes we must take leaps into the unknown and move into the darkness with anticipation and courage. Life is and will always be a beautiful balance of light and darkness. To feel the fullness of life we need to experience both.

Boldness has genius, power, and magic in it.

— Goethe

DAYBREAK

The happiest part of a man's life is what passes lying awake in bed in the morning.

—Samuel Adams

What is it that wakes you in the morning? Is it a jolting alarm, a pet eager for attention, a sleeping pill wearing off, or the soft beams of sunlight filtering into your room? It is wonderful to have the light of dawn be our alarm clock, for it is the way nature announces to all her creatures that another day has begun. Many of us do not give ourselves enough time in the morning to get ready for the day. We bound out of bed and immediately begin trying to fit too many activities into a brief time. A wonderful way to open the gift of a fresh new morning is to stay in bed a few minutes longer in order to think about the many surprises and adventures the day will bring. These extra daybreak moments allow us to peacefully prepare for the next twenty-four hours, and they also give us a moment to reflect on the blessings of each new day.

For today and its blessings, I owe the world an attitude of gratitude.

—Anonymous

DISTRACTIONS

*God, the master of time, never gives the future. He gives
only the present, moment by moment.*

—The Cloud of Unknowing

Our clocks and calendars drive us ever forward. What will I prepare
for the next meal? When will I have the oil changed in the car? When
should I make the appointment to see the dentist? The more time we
spend filling up our minutes and our days, the less we allow our mind
to rest in the present moment, which is the only moment we ever
really have. It takes a great deal of discipline and willpower to stay in
the "here and now." It takes concentration to focus on the person we
are talking to on the phone, the pet we are brushing, or the plant we
are watering. If we do not bring ourselves continuously back to the
present moment, our lives will be consumed with making plans for
events that may not even take place. Sometimes it helps to start small,
dedicating a few minutes throughout a day to "being in the present."
Life is too short to miss a moment of it, but we will if we do not
commit ourselves to being in this moment, and only this moment.

*The secret of health for both mind and body is not to
mourn for the past, not to worry about the future, or not
to anticipate troubles, but to live the present moment
wisely and earnestly.*

—The Buddha

THE DOLDRUMS

True life is lived when tiny changes occur.

—Leo Tolstoy

The doldrums are areas in the Atlantic Ocean sandwiched between the northern and southern hemispheres. They are hot, sticky, low-pressure areas with little wind. Ships that enter these places often come to a complete stop. Even though we might live thousands of miles from this region, we can slide into the doldrums. These are days when we completely lose our momentum and would prefer to sit and do absolutely nothing. We may not feel terribly blue or down—we have simply lost our energy and ability to move forward. It is all right to allow ourselves a few hours or even a day within this zone, but if the malaise persists we need to exert effort and gently pull ourselves out of this listlessness. It might help to set a small goal or task for the start of the next day. An interesting activity will prompt you to get up and dressed. You also might want to see where you can add variety to your life: maybe going out for breakfast or even buying a new plant that will need your care. The doldrums can attack anyone at any time, and when they do, don't panic, just remember to begin to move one small step at a time.

If you have inner peace, the external problems do not affect your deep sense of tranquillity. You are happy regardless of circumstance.

—The Dalai Lama

ECHO

From listening comes wisdom.

—Italian Proverb

Echo was one of the loveliest of the Greek wood nymphs, but she had one irritating fault: she was a chatterer. Echo loved the sound of her voice, and so day in and day out, she rarely listened to others. One day, Hera had enough of these one-way conversations and decided to teach Echo an important lesson. She took away Echo's ability to start a conversation and only allowed her to repeat what another person had said. Heartbroken, Echo disappeared and hid in secluded rocky areas and dark deep caves. This sad but lovely story can teach us two important things: First, even though we have interesting things to relate, we must not monopolize a conversation. Second, the listener has the most important role, for he/she must give undivided attention to the speaker. Conversations bring us together; sharing ideas and daily events creates a strong bond. This cannot happen if we do not remember Echo's lessons.

Nature gave us one tongue and two ears so we could hear twice as much as we speak.

—Epictetus

ENCHANTMENT

All the way to heaven is heaven.

—Saint Catherine of Siena

Enchantment means to be placed under a magic spell, and what better way than to be surrounded by the glorious sound of medieval Gregorian chants or the chants of Tibetan Buddhist monks? Lama Anagarika Govinda describes the chants of Buddhist monks as "sounds that seem to come from the womb of the earth or from the depth of space like rolling thunder." This is probably why more and more people are drawn to this music, for it casts a spell and takes them away from their normal daily affairs. Chants not only enchant us, but they also heal us. In a monastery in southern France, monks who had chanted from six to eight hours a day had this time reduced by several hours. In a short time the monks became more and more fatigued, and some became ill. They tried to get more rest and sleep, but that did not help. They called in a doctor who changed their diet; still the monks were listless. Finally someone suggested that they be allowed to return to their normal hours of chanting, and within a few months they were all energetic and well again. We all need enchantment in our lives, and we must be diligent in our search for it, because it will bring not only peace but also magic.

Music is said to be the speech of angels. It brings us to the infinite.

—Thomas Carlyle

ENTHUSIASM

Exuberance is beauty.

—William Blake

The word *enthusiasm* comes from the ancient Greek and means "possessed by a god." What a wonderful way to describe the passion and fervor we see in some people as they move through life. The zeal they embody is directed to every task, big or small, enjoyable or not. When we are around enthusiastic people we are pulled into their energy and find ourselves energized by their joy. It is easy to be enthusiastic about things we enjoy, but when we are forced to participate in things we do not like, it is easy to lose our enthusiasm. Some people may have been born with a larger fund of enthusiasm, but it is a trait we can all foster. Next time you find yourself having to do something you prefer not to do, be enthusiastic, even if it is an act. Sometimes when we display a certain attribute, we actually begin to feel that way. We can ill afford to miss moments of happiness because we do not live our lives in an enthusiastic and passionate way.

Catch on fire with enthusiasm and people will come for miles to see you burn.

—John Wesley

ESSENCE

Insist on yourself; never imitate.
—Ralph Waldo Emerson

The essence of something is its most important attribute—the summation of all its parts. It is what makes a person unique from all others in the world. In Aramaic the word *Alaha* means "God" as well as "essence" and "life force." We believe we can smell the essence of a flower in perfume and taste the essence of fruit in a drink. In Tibetan Buddhism there is a practice called *Chud len* or "essence extraction." It enables one to live on the essence of a flower, rock, or stick. Some Buddhist nuns and monks literally exist on a spoonful of finely ground rock or wood boiled in water. It is believed that the essence of the plant or mineral is able to pass on its energy to the person who takes it into their body. When you are near someone you can feel his or her essence: calm, happy, patient, resentful, or jealous. Each of us has our own unique essence. What is your individual essence? What do you want your essence to be? How can you nurture that essence today?

Know yourself and your neighbor will not mistake you.
—Scottish Proverb

EXCALIBUR

Not the glittering weapon fights the fight, but rather the hero's heart.

—Proverb

In legends and myths we have many stories of how heroes through wit and strength were able to fulfill ancient prophecies and become conquerors and kings. One of these stories is about Excalibur, the magical sword of King Arthur. Legend has it that it was embedded in a large stone and the people of England believed the man who could extract it would be their next ruler. Young Arthur through strength and intelligence released it and was thus proclaimed king of the Britons. In Greek history there is a similar story about the Gordian Knot. It was believed that a peasant devised an ingenious knot to tie his ox yoke to his chariot and the man who could untie it would be master of the entire world. When Alexander the Great passed through Gordian on his eastward path of conquest, he stopped in the city to see if he could fulfill the prophecy. Rather than attempting to untie the knot, he simply raised his sword and severed it. He then proclaimed himself the ruler of the entire world. Two leaders, two swords, and two feats of magical proportion are contained within these stories. In our modern world we seem to have fewer and fewer heroes/leaders endowed with selflessness, courage, creativity, wit, and wisdom. Who were your heroes as a child, and who are your heroes today? What did your childhood heroes teach you about honor, compassion, truth, and honesty? What values do your current heroes possess? Are the values you admire in these heroes ones that you embody? Are you someone's hero?

It is the deed that matters not the fame.

—German Proverb

EXPECTATIONS

*Human beings, by changing inner attitudes of their
minds, can change the outer aspect of their lives.*
                                    —William James

Some of our biggest disappointments in life probably took place
because we had an expectation that was not met. It may have been a
childhood birthday gift we had anticipated but did not receive, a
teenage wish to be accepted into a certain school or university, or an
adult relationship or job we sought but did not receive. Humans
spend their lives searching for happiness only to be disappointed over
and over again because they believe people or situations have let them
down. We simply need to shift our focus and realize that happiness
cannot depend on our getting our own way or having all our expectations met. True happiness does not come from outside sources but
from within.

*Happiness is a butterfly which, when pursued, is always
just beyond your grasp, but which, if you sit down quietly,
may alight on you.*
                                    —Nathaniel Hawthorne

FAITH

Where there is doubt, faith.
Where there is despair, hope.

—Prayer of St. Francis

When despair starts to descend upon us, we feel its crushing weight and doubt our ability to be able to lift it off our shoulders. Probably the two best antidotes for this dark and haunting feeling are faith and hope. We have seen many bowed down by loss and disappointment, and we have also seen that the passage of time and the help of others have allowed them to exit from this tunnel of discouragement. This should give us hope that we too can untangle ourselves from the grasp of despair. Linked with hope is faith in a higher power, nature, family, or close friends. Each of us has a safety net that will catch us when we think all is lost. Our task is to realize that we must reach out and seize the hand of a loved one or God so we can move into the light of understanding that faith and hope bring into our lives.

> *. . . let faith and hope be the atmosphere which man breathes in.*

—William James

FAMILY NAMES

*Every time we call something by its name, we make it
more real, like saying the name of a friend.*
—Thich Nhat Hanh

Ten centuries ago our names would have been simply Maria,
Katherine, Robert, Juan, or David. As time went on, however, there
were too many Edwards and Anns, so an additional descriptor was
needed: the David whose father is John, the Mary who lives by the
ditch, or the Richard who is a baker or clerk. Slowly surnames developed. When our ancestors came to this country, many had their
names changed by clerks at Ellis Island and other ports of entry. Other
names were altered by the indecipherable penmanship of a family
member or created by a slave owner assigning European last names to
his new slaves. Many of our ancestors' last names have been lost
because of adoption or the tradition of women giving up their maiden
names when they marry. We are lucky if we know three or four ances-
tral names, and probably only a few of these are the original medieval
names. Regardless of their historical accuracy, family names have great
meaning, for they are the thread that reaches far back and connects us
with the George who was the carpenter or the Sarah whose father was
a farmer. We are all chapters in the story of a bloodline, and it is wise
to remember and honor those who came before us.

There is history in all men's lives.
—William Shakespeare

FAMILY TREE

Some of us are fortunate to have an extensive genealogy of our families; others may feel lucky if they know the names of two of their grandparents. Even though we might not know the names of all our family members, each limb and branch of our family tree is part of us and gives us a sense of belonging to something larger than our own existence. Perhaps this is why ancestor worship is an important part of many cultures' spiritual beliefs. Have you ever taken old photographs and looked into the faces of your relatives? Have you searched the pictures for your eyes, your nose, your cheekbones? Do you know from whom you inherited your patience or your fiery temper? What questions would you like to ask one of these ancestors? What questions do you think they would like to ask you?

Never forget the importance of history. To know nothing of what happened before you took your place in the world is to remain a child forever.
—Anonymous

FEELINGS

It is terribly amusing how many climates of feelings one can go through in a day.

—Anne Morrow Lindbergh

What are you feeling at this very moment? Be still and listen to what is going on inside you. What thoughts are going through your mind? How does your body feel? Sometimes when we can't quite catch a feeling, drawing or doodling can make it come into focus. Drawing or writing about our feelings allows us to catch and release them. The frustrating thing about emotions is that when they remain unidentified they float aimlessly through our bodies and minds. It is not an easy task to go within yourself and search out the feelings bringing you discomfort and pain, but it is one of the best ways to bring peace and calm into your life.

I'm boiling with rage. . . . I'd like to stamp my feet, scream, give Mommy a good shaking, cry, and I don't know what else. . . . But still the brightest spot of all is that at least I can write down my thoughts and feelings, otherwise I would be absolutely stifled!

—Anne Frank

FETISHES

The world will never starve for want of wonders; but only for want of wonder.

—G. K. Chesterton

The most exquisite Native American stone and shell animal fetishes are carved in the Zuni Pueblo in New Mexico. Many tourists and collectors purchase these tiny objects and do not understand their power or sacredness. Anthropologists believe fetishes have always been part of the lives of these people, for they have been found in many southwestern prehistoric archaeological sites. Pueblo Indians believe the small stone carvings contain the power and attributes of the animal they represent. Because of their sacred powers, the fetishes are tenderly cared for and even fed blue cornmeal in the special container where they are housed. Many outsiders see this as a quaint superstition. However, most of us through the years have accumulated special artifacts that we would never part with because they contain the essence of something we value. In their own way, these items are sacred. We need these sacred objects, for they make us feel protected and bring comfort to our lives.

To comprehend something means to pick it up and love it. There is no other way to understand something.

—Thich Nhat Hanh

FINAL WORDS

The art of dying follows as a corollary from the art of living.

—Gandhi

As Gandhi was walking to a prayer meeting on January 30, 1948, a young man jumped out of the crowd and fired point-blank into his heart. Gandhi's frail body sank to the ground, and the holy phrase he had used all of his life came softly from his lips, "Rama, Rama, Rama" ("God, God, God"). Two days prior to his assassination, he had said, "If I am to die by the bullet of a madman, I must do this smiling. There must be no anger in me. God must be in my heart and on my lips." Like Gandhi, many great men and women have died with final words that encapsulated their lives. George Washington whispered, "It is well, I die hard, but I am not afraid to go." Emily Dickinson died with the remark "The fog is rising." "What is the question? What is the question? If there is no question, there is no answer," sighed Gertrude Stein. Leo Tolstoy departed with the words, "To seek, always to seek." Appropriately, "Drink to me" were Pablo Picasso's final words. Many great people of the world have died as they have lived, and fittingly their final moments and words were as inspiring as their lives.

Why are you weeping, did you think I was immortal?

—Final words of Louis XIV

FIREFLIES

Why we are like fireflies, too . . . traveling with our own
built-in illuminations . . . .

       —Paul Scott, *The Day of the Scorpion*

Fireflies are one of the most magical gifts of nature. As these tiny creatures dart about, children try to capture and enclose their radiant
bodies in glass containers so they can solve the riddle of their flicker-
ing glow. We are a lot like fireflies, for we all have a light within us and
we can see this light in others when we look into their eyes.
Sometimes the light is brilliant; other times it is dim and looks as if it
might go out. Many say the eyes are the windows of the soul, and if
this is true we must look carefully through these windows to see if
someone is in need of assistance or encouragement. We can light up
the corners of our world by sharing our inner light. This can be passed
from person to person as easily as people holding unlit candles can
pass a glowing flame from one to another, both keeping the light and
passing it on. A room lit with only one small flame can become luminous when we start sharing our light.

> *As the sun illuminates the moon and the stars, so let us*
> *illumine one another.*
>
>   —Anonymous

FOOTPRINTS

Immortality will come to such as are fit for it, and he who would be a great soul in the future must be a great soul now.

—Ralph Waldo Emerson

Outside the small foothill community of Morrison, Colorado, there is a ridge embedded with the footprints of creatures that lived more than 100 million years ago. One day an *Iguanodontids* dinosaur was walking through the muddy swampland and stepped into a particularly soggy part of the terrain, leaving a footprint we can still see and touch today. This ancient dinosaur was certainly unaware of the significance of this one step out of the thousands it took in its life. However, this one step was left as its legacy. We also have taken thousands of steps in our lifetimes. The wobbly steps of infancy and the exuberant exploring steps of young adulthood created some of our important footprints. Lasting prints, however, were left because of how we treated others and our world. As we continue down our path we must be aware that we still have time to leave significant footprints that will record our deeds and our actions. Some of these will be around hundreds if not thousands of years and will show others the manner in which we lived.

Tomorrow is endless.

—Russian Proverb

THE FOUNTAIN OF YOUTH

It is not with muscle, speed, or physical dexterity that great things are achieved but by reflection, force of character, and judgment; in these qualities old age is usually not only not poorer, but is even richer.

—Cicero

The Spanish explorer Ponce de Leon believed that hidden in the wilderness of Florida was a miraculous spring that would grant him his wish for eternal youth. When he explored this area he did find a spring of sparkling clear water and drank from it—and to his amazement nothing changed. Not one wrinkle vanished, and not one inch off his waist disappeared. For years he had searched, and now he had to accept the inevitable changes that aging brings. Most of us are amazed that an intelligent man like Ponce de Leon, who was raised in an advanced and sophisticated culture, could possess such superstitious beliefs. In our society, however, many individuals chase in an equally bizarre manner an elixir that will reverse the aging process. For them "the fountain of youth" might be found in wrinkle cream, tummy tucks, or hair replacement. It is true that we can outwardly erase some of the signs of aging, but it is fortunate that our inner age cannot be removed, for here is found the radiant, wise beauty gained through years of experience and adventures.

Birds sing after a storm; why shouldn't people feel as free to delight in whatever remains in them?

—Rose Fitzgerald Kennedy

GEESE

Alone we can do so little; together we can do so much.

—Helen Keller

When we look into a bright fall sky, we often catch the magnificent sight of a flock of geese flying south to their winter home. They create a perfect feathered triangle, and if you listen carefully you can actually hear their song. The magic of this "V" formation goes beyond its visual beauty, for geese in flight are one of the most perfect support systems in the natural world. Flying together rather than going solo adds 71 percent to their flying range. The inflight song you may detect is actually the flock honking encouragement to those up front, who have the most difficult job. When one goose gets sick or is wounded and sinks to the earth, two friends will follow it down in order to protect it. They will stay close by until it dies or is able to fly again. We would like to think that our lives are lived with such altruistic goals, but we often allow our self-interest to get in the way of always being there for others. Let us not be too proud to be willing to listen to the world of nature and learn the important lessons these wild ones can teach us.

When he took the time to help the man up the mountain, lo, he scaled it himself.

—Anonymous

GEMS

When we visualize a diamond or a ruby, we see a magnificent faceted stone placed in a beautifully crafted setting. When a ruby or diamond is pried from its prehistoric home, however, it has a far different appearance. There is a special beauty in these uncut stones, for as we hold them in our hands we know that deep within them there is a light waiting to be released. The light that dwells inside a stone is called *scintilla* in Latin; it is like the stone's soul, the source of its vitality. We often refer to a person who has not found his or her path or goal as a "diamond in the rough." The expression implies that within this individual is a *scintilla*, a most beautiful light filled with energy, just waiting to be released.

An ordinary human being is a lump of matter weighing between 50 and 100 kilograms. The living matter is the same matter of which the rest of the earth, the sun and even the most distant stars and nebulae are made.

—Julian Huxley

GEODES

Only God understands the universe.
—German Proverb

Geodes are the tiniest crystal caves found on this planet. They started as cavities in limestone and shale, and over millions of years precipitation seeped into the holes and minerals dissolved, creating fantastic quartz-lined geodes. Cracking open a geode is an adventure into an unknown territory, for your eyes are the first to behold the wonders of this geological miracle. There are many things in a single day that we can be the first and only ones to see: the juicy insides of an orange, peas nestled in their pod, or fresh moist kernels of corn as you strip back their husks. We miss so many miracles because we move too quickly through our daily chores and duties. Slow down and be an explorer in your own small world.

Simply behold the radiance of all.
—Joseph Campbell

GEOGRAPHY

Some memories are realities and are better than anything that can ever happen again.

—Willa Cather, *My Antonia*

How many places have you lived? How many houses have you called home? Close your eyes and place an imaginary globe in front of your mind's eye. Now start drawing lines that connect all these places. Because America is a mobile nation, few of us have stayed in one place our entire lives, much less are currently living in the house in which we were raised. The rest of the world's people, however, are more stationary and probably find our habit of packing up and moving out perplexing. There are certainly advantages to both lifestyles. Mobility brings new and interesting experiences and opens our minds to new and different ways of thinking and living. The settled lifestyle allows individuals to sink their roots deeply into the ground and learn the nature of a place and the people who live there. Every spot on the map that we have lived has taught us something new; it has challenged our worldview and allowed us to encounter others who may not think the way we do. Go back now to your imaginary map. At each location you have called home, come up with one thing this location taught you that is still valuable to you today.

Where we love is home, home that our feet may leave, but not our hearts.

—Oliver Wendell Holmes

GIFTS

Gift giving is a celebration that unites giver and receiver.
The bond is gratefulness.

—Br. David Steindl-Rast

The best part about gifts is giving them. When we select a present for a friend or family member, we have the opportunity to hold that person in our mind and heart as we search for the perfect gift. During this time we get to think about all their wonderful attributes and then hopefully discover something that fits the part of them we love the most. Too often we do not take enough time to concentrate deeply on the ones we love, and the selection and giving of gifts allow us to do that. It is fun to be present when the gift is unwrapped and to see the smile of appreciation and hear them say, "You know me so well." Gift giving gives us an opportunity to connect our hearts with the hearts of those we love.

He gave me a peach. Then I gave him an emerald
Not to pay him back, but to make our love long-lasting.
He gave me a plum. Then I gave him a black jade
Not to pay him back, but to make our love long-lasting.

—Chinese Poem, *The Book of Songs*

GLOBETROTTING

The world is a traveler's inn.

—Afghan Saying

On rainy days when schoolchildren must stay inside, they often play the game of "spin the globe." One student gives the globe a quick spin, and then another shuts his or her eyes and brings the globe to a halt. All the children then hover around to see where the person's finger landed, for it is hoped that they will visit it at some time in their lives. The lucky ones land in exotic places like Samarkand, Cuzco, Klostermansfeld, Katma Hora, or even Fuyang. Some of these young players will grow up to be globetrotters determined to make it to the exact place where their young finger landed many years ago. Others will be happy to learn about these exotic and faraway places by reading travel magazines and books. Whether we turn out to be globetrotters or armchair travelers, the twirl of a globe shows us there is more in this world than Iowa or New Hampshire. This model of our planet opens a window that allows us to realize that there are billions of people in the world just like us, dreaming similar dreams and going through their daily tasks with hopes for health and happiness. We must strive to see our planet as a global village where we are responsible for all our fellow citizens.

I observe myself to come to know others.

—Lao Tze

THE GOLDEN MEAN

Nothing to excess.

—engraved by the Seven Wise Men on the Temple to Apollo,
Delphi, Greece

In ancient Greece, mathematicians and philosophers explored the principle of the "golden mean." Mathematicians believed its formula would allow them to construct the perfect building. Philosophers also searched for this ideal but not within a mathematical framework. Aristotle applied it to the stages of a person's life. He felt the golden mean occurred at mid-life, a time of balance between the exuberance of youth and the serenity of age. Aristotle did not want to foster the naïve optimism of the young but instead to warn that aging could make many preoccupied with the losses it brings. He encouraged his fellow senior citizens to maintain the mirth of youth, which would balance the pessimism older people often feel. It is consoling to know that 2,300 years ago Aristotle was guiding his friends through the identical concerns we have about aging in the twenty-first century. Today, as then, our task is to search for the balance between optimism and pessimism, excess and frugality, security and risk taking, in order to find the balance point, which is the the golden mean.

The best and safest thing is to keep a balance in your life, acknowledge the great powers around us and in us. If you can do that, and live that way, you are really a wise man.

—Euripedes

THE GOLDEN RULE

Regard your neighbor's gain as your gain, and your neighbor's loss as your own loss.

—Tai Shang Kan Yin P'ien

Christianity
"Do unto others as you would have them do unto you." (Luke 6:31)

Buddhism
"Hurt not others with that which pains yourself." (Udanavarga 5:18)

Confucianism
"Is there any one maxim which ought to be acted throughout one's whole life? Surely the maxim of loving kindness is such. Do not unto others what you would not they should do unto you." (Analects 15:23)

Islam
"No one is a believer until he loves for his brother what he loves for himself." (Tradition)

Hinduism
"This is the sum of duty; do naught to others which if done thee, would cause thee pain." (Mahabharata 2:5-7)

Judaism
"What is hurtful to yourself do not to your fellow man. That is the whole of the Torah and the remainder is but commentary. Go learn it." (The Talmud)

What stirs your anger when done to you by others, that do not to others.

—Socrates

THE GOOD SAMARITAN

Teach us to live our ordinary lives with extraordinary love.

—Fr. Thomas Keating

The Good Samaritan is a biblical story about a compassionate traveler who came to the aid of a Jewish man left on the side of the road to die. Many people do not realize that at this time, the Jews and the Samaritans, although living in close proximity, harbored a deep and longstanding prejudice against each other. This is a story of tolerance, for here we have an account told by Jesus of Nazareth, a Jew, about a Samaritan who risked a great deal to aid a neighbor who was considered his enemy. No one saw the Samaritan giving aid and comfort; he did not do it to gain honor or anyone's gratitude. He did it because that is what one individual does for another. It is sometimes hard to find the Good Samaritans in our midst, for their contributions are often made privately and go without recognition. Many of us are kind and generous, but we also like others to know about our good deeds. How many Good Samaritans have assisted you? What Good Samaritan acts have you performed without seeking honor or recognition?

A tree is known by its fruit; man by his deed. A good deed is never lost; he who sows courtesy reaps friendship, and he who plants goodness gathers love.

—St. Basil

THE GRAIL

What is to give light must endure the burning.
—Viktor Frankl

The Holy Grail has been a mystery for more than 2,000 years. Some believe it was a priceless jewel, others that it was a possession of Seth, the child of Adam and Eve. The most common belief, however, is that the Grail was the cup Jesus and his disciples drank from at the Last Supper. One legend continues this story by telling how Joseph of Arimathea took the Grail to Glastonbury, England, where he founded a monastery. Joseph was the man who after the crucifixion of Christ donated his tomb for Jesus' burial. We also associate the Grail with King Arthur and his knights Perseval, Galahad, and Bors, who went on a quest for this holy relic. This search is a story about loyalty, stamina, and heroism, for when they departed from Camelot they vowed to risk everything to retrieve this sacred object. The Grail has become an important legend, a symbol of the quest into the unknown mysteries of life that we all undertake. However, only the brave, the loyal, and those filled with faith complete the inward journey to self-knowledge. The reward for going on a Grail search is that an unknown becomes known and wisdom is gained because of the willingness to venture into the dangerous uncharted territory in search of our true natures.

People say that what we're all seeking is a meaning for life. I don't think that's what we're really seeking. I think that what we're seeking is an experience of being alive.
—Joseph Campbell

GROWTH

Everything changes, nothing remains without change.
—The Buddha

It is fun to watch the growth of chicks, puppies, and human babies. It is so gradual that one often doesn't notice the immense changes that are taking place until one is out of touch for a week or two. Part of us would like to keep babies as infants, but their development is so natural and each stage is so exciting that we would never truly want them to stay one age. As we get older, we also see and feel significant transformations in our bodies, memories, and strength. We may believe the changes we experience in the second half of life are not positive or exciting, but that is because we fail to recognize the inner growth taking place. If we look carefully at these transformations, we will see that our feelings of empathy for others are greater and that we have a deeper understanding of the events surrounding us. What a wonderful realization it is to discover that we are still growing, maturing, and ripening.

Each blade of grass has its Angel that bends over it and whispers, Grow, Grow.
—The Talmud

HALOES

Love must be as much a light as a flame.

—Henry David Thoreau

Luminous haloes surround the images of holy people, saints, and angels in the artwork of most religious traditions. The sacred space around the bodies seems to shimmer and cast out a glow just as a lit candle throws beams of light into dark corners. Many people believe we all have auras around our bodies that vary in color and intensity. Some gifted healers can see this light and use it in their healing practice. We all know people who seem to be lit from within and who are able to cast this light of caring and compassion to all those around them. We all have a light within us, but many keep it hidden because they do not believe it is really there or because they are afraid to share it with others. We know how wonderful it is to be enlightened by another, and we also must be willing to allow our light to shine forth in a caring and healing way.

I light the lamp of wisdom and dispel all darkness from the world.

—Bhagavad Gita

HEADLINES

The unexpected often happens.

—Plato

Many mornings when we read our newspaper the headlines announce an event that will alter the course of our lives. If you had the power to change one headline that has occurred in history, what headline would it be? Here are some possible changes:

Japanese Turned Back Before Pearl Harbor Is Attacked
Cure for Aids Discovered
Plot to Assassinate President Lincoln Uncovered
Hitler Defeated in Poland

It is hard to know what chain of events might be created by our new headlines. When you change one event in history, other events immediately change or disappear. This activity shows the impact one historical moment can have on the world and how it can change the course of our lives.

The causes of the events are even more interesting than the events themselves.

—Thomas Carlyle

HIDDEN MOTIVES

Be suspicious of yourself! Inquire about your hidden motives. It takes courage to repent, and more courage to change.

—Rumi

So often conflicts arise in our relationships because we have a personal agenda that we want others to accept. In order to make that happen, we manipulate the situation in order to get our way. Often our motives come from old unconscious habits that are hidden not only from others, but also from ourselves. Next time you find yourself manipulating a person or a situation, see if you can detect what prompted you to try to control what is taking place. Change can occur if we accurately see what is transpiring and then make a commitment to alter the behavior. Bringing motives out of hiding will benefit not only ourselves but also all those who have been frustrated by our past manipulations.

That which we understand we cannot blame.

—Goethe

HIDING PLACES

I'm hiding, I'm hiding,
And no one knows where
For all they can see is my
Toes and my hair.

—Dorothy Aldis

All creatures have hiding places: tiny ocean fish glide into the forests of coral reefs, badgers disappear deep into their tunnels, cats find a corner under a bed, and children bury themselves under mounds of blankets. Other creatures disappear because they can camouflage themselves; even though they are in the open the predator thinks they have vanished. We all need a hiding place so we can vanish momentarily to think through something, shed a secret tear, say a prayer, or have a moment of silence. Do you have a hiding place? If not, search for one. It is a place that will guard your secrets and keep you safe.

The right to be left alone is indeed the beginning of all freedom.

—Justice William O. Douglas

HOLOGRAMS

I know nothing else but miracles.

—Walt Whitman

When we stop believing in miracles, we must remember what holograms teach us about our miraculous bodies. A hologram is created through a complex scientific procedure that uses laser beams to produce three-dimensional images that one can walk straight through or even view from above or below. The difficult thing to understand about a hologram is that every tiny piece of the hologram contains within it the entire image that we can see. This same principle is true of our bodies. Scientific discoveries have shown that every cell, whether it is found in our stomach, brain, or eye, contains a copy of our entire master DNA blueprint and has within it enough information to create us entirely from scratch. We take for granted our fingers, taste buds, and ability to digest large particles of food. We often forget we are waking, walking, talking miracles!

The final mystery is oneself . . .

—Oscar Wilde

HOMECOMING

*Your treasure house is within you. It holds all you will
ever need.*

—Hui-Hai

In how many houses, apartments, condominiums, or cabins have you lived in your life? It is fun to recall all of these homes and try to remember the neighborhoods in which each dwelling was located. What was your favorite home? What was your favorite room? Sometimes when we recall a special moment we can immediately visualize the room in which it took place. Some loved places from our childhood were the dining room where we had Thanksgiving dinner; the bedroom where we told our secrets to our closest friends; the basement or attic filled with mysterious corners; or the bathroom where we had warm and sudsy bubble baths. Do you have one special object that has always moved with you? If so, it has probably given you a sense of familiarity as you moved from place to place. With many moves our lives can lose a sense of continuity, so it is important to find a thread that keeps all these places connected. We also must remember that home is wherever our hearts feel open and filled with peace.

*Does one really have to fret
About enlightenment?
No matter what road I travel,
I'm going home.*

—Shinsho

HONESTY

The largest amount of cash ever found and returned to its owners was $240,000 in unmarked $10 and $20 bills found in a street in Los Angeles by Douglas William Johnston in March 1961. He received many letters of which 25 percent suggested he was crazy.

—Guinness Book of Records

Most of us see ourselves as honest individuals, and yet it is always surprising to run into someone who seems to be honest beyond a fault. This is the person who at the checkout line returns just a few pennies to a clerk who undercharged him, or the person who would never tell a white lie even to save herself embarrassment. These people have set the highest of standards for themselves and have become impeccably honest. Some might think that they are too nice or too naïve, but these individuals would respond that it makes no difference whether the situation is large or small: the principle of honesty must not be compromised. It is important to look at our personal level of honesty. Are we honest only if it makes us look good? Are we honest when we know doing otherwise would hurt another person? Are we honest 99.9 percent of the time because that is a principle we believe in deeply? Are there changes you would like to make in the area of your honesty?

A crooked stick will have a crooked shadow.

—African Proverb

HUMMINGBIRDS

As a child I could not understand why I should pray for human beings only. When my mother had kissed me goodnight, I used to add a silent prayer that I had composed for all living things.

—Albert Schweitzer

Many people are fond of animals, but it seems that the bigger the creature the more regard human beings give it. Whales, elephants, grizzly bears, and king cobras are greatly respected, and communities come together to protect them and preserve their environments. The smaller the creature, the less attention and protection we provide. We see children gleefully stomping tiny ants, and we watch prairie dogs become victims of target practice. It is doubtful that at the time of creation there was a hierarchy based on size. If we look closely at some of the smallest creatures, we will find the most incredible attributes. For example, the wee hummingbird that weighs less than one marshmallow can fly 25 miles an hour on the level and can double that speed on a dive. Its tiny wings beat 75 times a second, and when it travels back and forth across the Gulf of Mexico, which it loves to do, it will have to beat its wings four million times each way. All animals, regardless of their size and weight, help keep our planet running in an orderly and efficient way. If it were not for the ladybug, our gardens would be devoured, and if it were not for butterflies and hummingbirds, our flowers would not be pollinated. No matter what size or shape, we are all necessary ingredients in this flourishing, flowing planet.

What is man without beasts? If all the beasts were gone, man would die from a great loneliness of spirit.

—Chief Seattle

IDEALISM

It is not possible to flow backward while there is youth in the world.

—Helen Keller

In 491 BC, the legend goes, the armies of the Greek city-states met the mighty undefeated Persian army on the battlefield at Marathon. The Greeks knew the outcome of this battle would determine their future autonomy and freedom. Philippides, a fleet-footed young Athenian soldier, had been given orders to race to Athens to tell the citizens the outcome of the battle the moment it was decided. When the Athenians had triumphed, the weary soldier ran 26 hilly miles into the center of Athens. The legend says that at the foot of the Acropolis he gasped, "Victory," then collapsed and died. We cannot be sure of the historical accuracy of this story, but it does tell us much about the patriotism of this Athenian youth. The young people of America seem to be losing the idealism of Philippides. In a survey conducted during a recent election, it was discovered that probably only one-third of young voters would participate in the election. The youth of our country have become discouraged and cynical, and even though we might agree with some of their concerns, we also know we cannot afford to have any citizen drop out of the political process. All of us have some contact with young people, and we must find a way to help them understand how much their country needs their commitment and energy. What can you do to encourage a young person to see how essential he or she is to the future of our country?

No matter what our attempts to inform, it is our ability to inspire that will turn the tides.

—Syracuse Cultural Workers

IDLENESS

Nothing to do, nothing to force, nothing to want—
everything happens by itself.

—Lama Gendun Rinpoche

The word *idle* brings chills to some people. In our culture, which was founded on a strong work ethic, being idle implies that you are not doing your share of the work or even that you are a lazy individual. When asked what we did in one day, fearing disapproval, we rarely respond, "I did nothing." This is unfortunate, for we all need time simply to sit under a tree, swing in a hammock, or take a walk with no destination. Some people seem to have a gift of knowing how to be idle, and when we watch them relax and gain peace during these restful times, we know they are neither lazy nor bored. Learning to be idle takes time and discipline. Often when we start feeling the sweet mood of idleness descending, the old work habit bounces right up and off we dash to dust the house or pay the bills. Start practicing idleness one hour a week, and then if you can break old habits, increase this time. Don't feel guilty about these moments, for there is an *Idleness Guarantee* that states you will be brighter, healthier, more creative, and happier within a few short weeks.

If you have spent a perfectly useless afternoon in a per-
fectly useless manner, you have learned how to live.

—Lin Yufang

IMAGINATION

I never saw a purple cow,
I never hope to see one.
But I can tell you, anyhow
I'd rather see than be one.

—Gelett Burgess

Have you ever wondered what it would feel like to be the last autumn leaf to drop from a tree, a jack-o-lantern three days after Halloween, a tiny chick making its decision to break out of its egg? One of the most important characteristics of a creative mind is its ability to turn itself into something else. Many of the greatest inventions have come from this spontaneous process, and some of the world's greatest literature has been created because authors have been able to imagine themselves changed into an inanimate or animate object. As you move through your day, look for things that will spark your creativity. Ask yourself questions that stretch your imagination. How would it feel to be the unread newspaper, the mold on top of the leftovers in the refrigerator, the houseplants thirsty for a drink? If you are feeling creative, how would it feel to be a purple cow?

The world of reality has limits; the world of imagination
is boundless.

—Jean-Jacque Rousseau

INSPIRATION

Love your beliefs and you can turn the world around.
—Henry David Thoreau

The word "inspiration" comes from the Latin *inspirare*, "filled with the spirit." We use this word to mean to breathe in air and to indicate when something or someone has a compelling influence on our life. In every age there have been philosophers and sages who have helped people move to new levels of thinking and spirituality: Socrates, Lao Tze, Buddha, Jesus Christ, Mohammed, Albert Einstein, Mother Teresa. Each of us has our own personal sage and favorite philosophers. These are the people who taught us, consoled us, and helped us along our life path. We often breathe in their power, energy, and wisdom and are transformed by their presence in our lives. Which sages and philosophers have been most important in your life? How did they inspire you? Was it their actions or their words that influenced you the most? Inspiring people often pass on the art of inspiration. What difference do you make in other people's lives? Who has been inspired by your presence?

If you wish to know the road up the mountain, ask the man who goes back and forth on it.

—Zanrin

INTUITION

A moment's insight is sometimes worth a life's experience.
—Oliver Wendell Holmes

We often believe some people are more intuitive than we are, but in reality we all have the gift of intuition; some of us are simply more open and receptive. In order to cultivate intuition, we must dedicate time to quieting our minds and tuning into the open and receptive space inside of us. We must be nonjudgmental when intuition presents us with an idea we may feel is unreasonable or impractical. (Intuition is rarely rational or logical.) Many times we mistakenly believe our intuition has deserted us, but it is just that we must listen more carefully. Intuition may come as a small voice that gently whispers in your ear, or it may present itself as an electric jolt that literally turns lights on inside your head. Be open to it, play with it, and be willing to act on the messages it brings you.

Knowledge has three degrees—opinion, science, and illumination.

—Plotinus

JEALOUSY

In jealousy there is more self-love than love.
—Francois de La Rochefoucauld

We all know how destructive a jealous heart can be for our happiness as well as for our relationships. As children this feeling was usually unconscious but ever-present: "I was the one who wanted a new bike for Christmas!" or "I should have been the one chosen to be a cheerleader!" As we age, we are more conscious of our jealous feelings and can normally feel them as they start to rise up in our bodies. We still, however, do not always know how to control them. Sometimes jealousy shows when we do not ask our friends about their good fortune—a trip to Tahiti or a new condo on the lake. It is sometimes hard to understand that the happiness of other people will bring much joy into the world and thus make our own lives happier.

Jealousy knows no loyalty.
—Spanish Proverb

JOURNALS

Memory is the diary we all carry around with us.

—Oscar Wilde

Many of us have the best intentions of keeping a journal or diary, but they get lost in the rush and weariness of a day. We often regret not being disciplined when we are trying to remember a profound thought we had a year ago or the exact date a special event occurred. A journal doesn't have to be time-consuming, and it can take a simple form. It might be jotting notes in your weekly calendar. It could be your photo album or even a file folder for each year where you can tuck away clippings, photographs, greeting cards, and special correspondence. Often the joy and importance of a journal is not the moment of writing but the returning to it after many years have passed. Keeping a diary allows us to reenter past times with the wisdom and experience we have gained since we wrote the entry. Journals and diaries allow us to relive special moments in a new and startlingly fresh way.

Painting is another way of keeping a diary.

—Pablo Picasso

JOY

One joy scatters a hundred griefs.

—Chinese Proverb

When was the last time you:
Took a walk in the rain?
Licked a dewdrop off a leaf or pine needle?
Rode a merry-go-round?
Delivered an Easter basket?
Caught snowflakes on your tongue?
Got up five minutes before sunrise so you could see the sky's color
    before the sun peeked through?
Watched a spider spin a web?
Made a snow angel?
Played hopscotch?
Toasted marshmallows?

*All the animals, excepting man, know that the principal
business of life is to enjoy it.*

—Samuel Butler

JUDGMENTS

If you judge people, you have not time to love.

—Mother Teresa

One of the quickest thoughts that can flash across our minds is to pass judgment on another person: "That outfit is not becoming"; "That child needs to be more courteous"; "She has no sense of humor." Because these thoughts move at the speed of light, we often cannot get hold of them and stop them in their tracks. It is so easy to join in with others when they start to belittle another person. Often our feelings of inferiority or low self-esteem encourage us to make negative judgments so we can feel superior. Instead of spending time demeaning others, we should be helping ourselves overcome unhappy feelings. Whether judgments are made in public or kept as secrets in our hearts, they are more destructive to us than to the one we judge. When you next catch a judgment flashing through your mind, remember the sage advice given by Jesus of Nazareth more than 2,000 years ago: "And why beholdest thou the mote that is in thy brother's eye, but considerest not the beam that is in thy own eye?"

What hurt could it do thee if thou wouldst let it pass and make no accounts of it?

—Thomas à Kempis

JUSTICE

Nothing is preferred before justice.

—Socrates

Throughout the history of the world rulers and politicians have sought to impose justice on the land. Justice reflects the values of a culture, and thus it takes on many different appearances. As we look back on famous trials, we shake our heads in puzzlement at the findings of a legal system during a particular time in history. Socrates was put to death because he was determined to help the youth of Athens find truth. Jesus Christ was executed because of his revolutionary doctrine of loving others. Galileo spent the last years of his life under house arrest because of his theory that the earth was not the center of the universe. Each of us, in our own lives, must strive to treat all people with justice. Often our personal perspective, which is formed by our age, economic group, and ethnic background, interferes with our objectivity. We all know how filled with rage we can become when we are treated unfairly. We cannot afford to let our own needs, prejudices, or feelings make us blind to seeking justice for everyone.

It is much more difficult to judge oneself than to judge others.

—Antoine de Saint-Exupéry

KARMA

Whenever we act negatively, it leads to pain and suffering; whenever we act positively, it eventually results in happiness.

—Sogyal Rinpoche

In Hindu and Buddhist doctrine there is a principle called the law of karma. Westerners sometimes misunderstand the meaning of this mystical principle, even though it is one that is found in all religions of the world. St. Paul clearly stated this principle when he said, "Whatsoever a man soweth, that shall he also reap." It is the same as the physical law stating that for every action there is an equal and opposite reaction. The principle of karma simply means that for everything we do in our lives there is a consequence. If we are kind we will receive kindness; if we give love and compassion we will receive love and compassion. We can see this clearly in our lives, for when we hurt someone it often rebounds on us and we are the one who is truly hurt because of guilt and regret. The law of karma states that we can never escape from the consequences of our actions, but we are always given the opportunity to learn from our errors. It is so easy to deny our inappropriate behavior, but if we do, we will not be able to make the necessary corrections in order to restore good karma.

That which a man sacrifices is never lost.

—German Proverb

KINDNESS

My religion is kindness.

—The Dalai Lama

When asked how a man could become perfect, the medieval mystic Johan Ruysbroeck responded, "Be kind, be kind, be kind." Most of us feel a life committed to being a kind human is a wonderful goal but also impractical. We feel that sometimes we must be strong and assertive with others to accomplish what we need and want. We all, however, know individuals who move through life thinking of the needs of others before their own. Their kindness radiates out to the world every hour of the day. They possess an inner strength, for they have learned to control their negative reactions when others hurt them or behave inappropriately. Developing a caring heart takes practice. We must work on responding to sarcasm and rudeness with gentle kindness. We can transform our negative feelings and reactions if we just pay close attention to where our emotions may be taking us. Impatience and cruelty are not natural responses. Our human nature is one of kindness and of love.

A tree is known by its fruit; a man by his deeds. A good deed is never lost; he who sows it reaps friendship, and he who plants goodness gathers love.

—St. Basil

LABYRINTH

*As we find our meaning and purpose we also realize that
some invisible form of guidance has been leading us.*

—Lauren Artress

The symbol of a labyrinth has existed for millennia and has appeared in the art and religions of cultures around the world. We find it on the floor of medieval European cathedrals, in tattoos on the bodies of people who live in the South Sea Islands, in Sufi poetry, and in Celtic knots that adorn ancient European jewelry. The labyrinth is a sacred path, a metaphor for the wanderings we have taken in this life. We move from point to point on an inward journey to find a place of truth and peace, and then we must turn around and move out from the center so we can share our discoveries with others. This trip requires patience, an open and clear mind, and the most important thing—a faith that the trip into and out of the labyrinth will give us the wisdom we seek.

A man's courage is full of faith.

—Cicero

LASTING IMPRESSIONS

Waste no time talking about great souls and how they should be. Become one yourself!

—Marcus Aurelius

We have all met someone, even if the meeting was brief, who left a lasting impression on us. It may have been the compassion we could see deep within their eyes, their ability to articulate their deepest thoughts, or their radiant smile. By being in our presence they give us a gift of peace and wisdom we will never forget. We have all left lasting impressions on others; however, many times we are unaware that another has been deeply affected by something we did or said. What is one of your attributes that leaves a lasting impression on those you meet? Is it your creativity, sense of humor, friendliness, or ability to make people feel at home? We all leave imprints upon the world, and we must be sure they are ones that help others grow so they too will leave their lasting impressions on others.

Man is only truly great when he acts from his passion.

—Benjamin Disraeli

LAUGHTER

He deserves Paradise who makes his companions laugh.

—The Koran

What a gift it is to be able to laugh with others. We all know people who have the gift of making a room light up with giggles and chuckles. This special warmth spreads across space, for laughter is as contagious as a yawn. Scientists have discovered that laughter not only solidifies relationships but can actually lessen our perception of pain and discomfort. We have great need to laugh, for it not only floods our body with health but also assures us that we are not alone. Laughter is like a tickle; studies have proven you cannot tickle yourself, for you need the element of surprise and the gleeful warmth of another person by your side. Don't ever be afraid to give yourself over to the curing warmth of a good laugh shared with friends.

Those who bring sunshine to the lives of others cannot keep it from themselves.

—Anonymous

LEAVES

I have been treading on leaves all day until I am autumn tired.

—Robert Frost, *A Leaf Treader*

Many people do not live in areas that allow for walks in a wood through colored autumn leaves that crunch and crackle underfoot. Everyone, however, has had the opportunity through photographs or vacations to experience the descent of autumn on the land. Part of us rejoices in the breathtaking beauty of this season, but another part of us grieves to see it passing. We spend a year watching bare tree branches burst forth with tiny light green buds that change to mature full-grown leaves and then transform into a brilliant farewell before they drop to the ground. As we watch this transformation, we see how similar it is to our own life passage. When we accept this natural flowing cycle, we will be able to find peace, not sorrow, in endings.

There is no other door to knowledge than the door Nature opens; and there is no truth except the truth we discover in Nature.

—Luther Burbank

LEGACY

No legacy is so rich as honesty.
—William Shakespeare

What is the greatest legacy that was bequeathed to you? Was it the heirloom quilt made by your great-grandmother, the letters from an uncle who served in the trenches during World War I, or the principles of honesty and compassion your father passed on to you? From the time we are young adults, we start constructing the legacy we will pass on to the future. For what do you most want to be remembered? What will be your legacy?

We are born for love. It is the principle of existence, and its only end.
—Benjamin Disraeli

THE LOTUS

Every moment Nature starts on the longest journey, and
every moment she reaches her goal.

—Goethe

The lotus has been a special flower in many religions of the world as
well as in legends and fairy tales. We grew up looking at illustrations
in children's books showing tiny frogs happily napping on water lilies
or swans peacefully gliding among a garden of water flowers. We find
the lotus in Homer's *Odyssey* when the hero Odysseus visits Lotusland,
a place of contented idleness and delight. It is also found in Buddhism
as a symbol of purity and divine birth, which is why we often see the
Buddha sitting on a lotus in bloom. When we see a lily resting on a
pond, it appears to be floating freely on the water. If you dove beneath
the surface, however, you would find it tethered in the pond's soft,
very mud. In this murky darkness, it puts down its roots. We are
a lotus, rooted in darkness and yet always struggling upward to
the light of understanding, totally dependent on the four elements of earth, air, fire, and water.

To create a little flower is the labour of ages.

—William Blake

LETTERS

Even if you have nothing to write, write and say so.

—Cicero

Every day we open our mailboxes with anticipation, hoping we will
find more than just catalogs, bills, and bulk mailings. We quickly sort
through our bundle searching for a handwritten envelope with the
return address of someone we know and love. In our technological
age, e-mails are becoming the preferred way of communicating. It is
fun to find an e-mail waiting on our computer, but it is not the same
as opening our mailbox and discovering an unexpected letter. Letters
are precious gifts that reach across miles to touch hearts. To get letters
you must write letters. From whom would you love to hear? That is
the person you need to write today.

True friendship is like sound health; the value is seldom
known until it is lost.

—Chinese Proverb

LISTENING

Let the wise listen and gain wisdom and let the discerning get guidance.

—Proverbs 1:5

When was the last time someone listened to you? To be truly listened to is one of the greatest gifts one can receive. Too often when we are engaged in a conversation, the other person seems to be waiting to snatch the topic away so they can give their opinion or tell about their experiences. If you think about the last person who really listened to you, probably the most important thing he/she did was remain silent. Schools do an admirable job of teaching reading and speaking in public, but rarely do they teach students how to listen. Becoming an expert listener takes practice. Your nonverbal behavior is the most important thing because you are not going to be the one who is talking. Here are things to remember: Maintain eye contact even though the speaker might not want to look at you; be aware that your facial expressions, energy level, and posture show your interest. Put yourself in their shoes in order to perceive the feelings behind their words. Carefully listening to another is a special gift and one that you will find returned to you.

The most difficult thing of all is to keep quiet and listen.

—Aulus Gellius

LONGEVITY

The moral progress of mankind is due to the aged. The old grow better and wiser.

—Leo Tolstoy

At age 75, Disraeli resigned as Prime Minister of England for the second and last time.

At age 77, Mae West starred in *Myra Breckinridge.*

At age 79, Verdi wrote *Falstaff.*

At age 80, Grandma Moses had her first art show.

At age 83, Charlie Chaplin got an Oscar for *Limelight.*

At age 87, Frank Lloyd Wright proposed a one-mile-hi the city of Chicago.

At age 89, Bertrand Russell was put in prison for civil supporting the Campaign for Nuclear Disarma

At age 90, Will and Ariel Durant published volum *Civilization.*

At age 94, Leopold Stokowski signed a six-year

At age 96, Tesichi Igarachi climbed Mt. Fuji.

*I do not think seventy years is the
woman, nor that seventy millions is
woman, nor that years will ever ste
or anyone else.*

LOVE

If you wish to be loved; Love!

—Seneca

Some of us were raised in families where saying "I love you" was a part of daily life. Other families may feel deep love but are less demonstrative in their feelings. It is important to bring these words out into the open, even though they may make others a bit nervous or even embarrassed. Saying "I love you" is a way to thank another for being a vital part of your existence. We never know when life's circumstances will separate us from someone we love, so we must let people know how we feel when we still have the opportunity to be near them. How many times did you say "I love you" today?

Tell me who you love, and I'll tell you who you are.

—African Proverb

LOVING-KINDNESS

Compassion is not compassion unless it is active.

—Sogyal Rinpoche

Avalokiteshvara is the Buddha of Compassion. Paintings show him with 1,000 eyes so that he can see all the anguish that exists on the earth. He also has 1,000 arms so that he can reach out to all corners of the universe in order to alleviate pain. Every day we see people suffering and in need, yet we fail to reach out to them because we feel so helpless and inadequate. We may have the eyes of Avalokiteshvara to see the anguish, but we often do not stretch out our arms to give support and assistance. We cannot afford to ignore what we see or refuse to use our hearts and hands to give loving-kindness to those who are in need.

Love begets love.

—St. Teresa of Avila

LETTERS

Even if you have nothing to write, write and say so.

—Cicero

Every day we open our mailboxes with anticipation, hoping we will find more than just catalogs, bills, and bulk mailings. We quickly sort through our bundle searching for a handwritten envelope with the return address of someone we know and love. In our technological age, e-mails are becoming the preferred way of communicating. It is fun to find an e-mail waiting on our computer, but it is not the same as opening our mailbox and discovering an unexpected letter. Letters are precious gifts that reach across miles to touch hearts. To get letters you must write letters. From whom would you love to hear? That is the person you need to write today.

True friendship is like sound health; the value is seldom known until it is lost.

—Chinese Proverb

LISTENING

Let the wise listen and gain wisdom and let the discerning get guidance.

—Proverbs 1:5

When was the last time someone listened to you? To be truly listened to is one of the greatest gifts one can receive. Too often when we are engaged in a conversation, the other person seems to be waiting to snatch the topic away so they can give their opinion or tell about their experiences. If you think about the last person who really listened to you, probably the most important thing he/she did was remain silent. Schools do an admirable job of teaching reading and speaking in public, but rarely do they teach students how to listen. Becoming an expert listener takes practice. Your nonverbal behavior is the most important thing because you are not going to be the one who is talking. Here are things to remember: Maintain eye contact even though the speaker might not want to look at you; be aware that your facial expressions, energy level, and posture show your interest. Put yourself in their shoes in order to perceive the feelings behind their words. Carefully listening to another is a special gift and one that you will find returned to you.

The most difficult thing of all is to keep quiet and listen.

—Aulus Gellius

LONGEVITY

The moral progress of mankind is due to the aged. The old grow better and wiser.

—Leo Tolstoy

At age 75, Disraeli resigned as Prime Minister of England for the second and last time.

At age 77, Mae West starred in *Myra Breckinridge.*

At age 79, Verdi wrote *Falstaff.*

At age 80, Grandma Moses had her first art show.

At age 83, Charlie Chaplin got an Oscar for *Limelight.*

At age 87, Frank Lloyd Wright proposed a one-mile-high building for the city of Chicago.

At age 89, Bertrand Russell was put in prison for civil disobedience for supporting the Campaign for Nuclear Disarmament.

At age 90, Will and Ariel Durant published volume 11 of *The Story of Civilization.*

At age 94, Leopold Stokowski signed a six-year recording contract.

At age 96, Tesichi Igarachi climbed Mt. Fuji.

I do not think seventy years is the time of a man or woman, nor that seventy millions is the time of man or woman, nor that years will ever stop the existence of me, or anyone else.

—Walt Whitman

THE LOTUS

*Every moment Nature starts on the longest journey, and
every moment she reaches her goal.*

—Goethe

The lotus has been a special flower in many religions of the world as
well as in legends and fairy tales. We grew up looking at illustrations
in children's books showing tiny frogs happily napping on water lilies
or swans peacefully gliding among a garden of water flowers. We find
the lotus in Homer's *Odyssey* when the hero Odysseus visits Lotusland,
a place of contented idleness and delight. It is also found in Buddhism
as a symbol of purity and divine birth, which is why we often see the
Buddha sitting on a lotus in bloom. When we see a lily resting on a
pond, it appears to be floating freely on the water. If you dove beneath
the surface, however, you would find it tethered in the pond's soft,
watery mud. In this murky darkness, it puts down its roots. We are
like a lotus, rooted in darkness and yet always struggling upward to
find the light of understanding, totally dependent on the four elements of earth, air, fire, and water.

To create a little flower is the labour of ages.

—William Blake

LOVE

If you wish to be loved; Love!

—Seneca

Some of us were raised in families where saying "I love you" was a part of daily life. Other families may feel deep love but are less demonstrative in their feelings. It is important to bring these words out into the open, even though they may make others a bit nervous or even embarrassed. Saying "I love you" is a way to thank another for being a vital part of your existence. We never know when life's circumstances will separate us from someone we love, so we must let people know how we feel when we still have the opportunity to be near them. How many times did you say "I love you" today?

Tell me who you love, and I'll tell you who you are.

—African Proverb

LOVING-KINDNESS

Compassion is not compassion unless it is active.

—Sogyal Rinpoche

Avalokiteshvara is the Buddha of Compassion. Paintings show him with 1,000 eyes so that he can see all the anguish that exists on the earth. He also has 1,000 arms so that he can reach out to all corners of the universe in order to alleviate pain. Every day we see people suffering and in need, yet we fail to reach out to them because we feel so helpless and inadequate. We may have the eyes of Avalokiteshvara to see the anguish, but we often do not stretch out our arms to give support and assistance. We cannot afford to ignore what we see or refuse to use our hearts and hands to give loving-kindness to those who are in need.

Love begets love.

—St. Teresa of Avila

LOYALTY

Without loyalty, it is impossible to love.

—Eknath Easwaran

We all have friends and family members whose loyalty we would never doubt. We know they will be there when they are needed, that our needs are as important to them as their own, and that if called on they would give their lives for us. These people are precious to us and they give meaning and security to our daily existence. So many of our relationships, however, are conditional: "I will love you if you behave the way I want you to," or "I will care and protect you if you do not make mistakes." For friendships to be true there cannot be degrees of loyalty, for we must trust that our friends will not change their minds or disregard us when we need them. Trusting that a person will be there reassures us of their loyalty, which puts the stamp of love upon the relationship. We pray for loyal friends. How loyal a friend are you?

For whither thou goest, I will go.

—Ruth 1:16

A MAGIC CARPET

If a little dreaming is dangerous, the cure for it is not to dream more, but to dream all the time.

—Marcel Proust

Pretend that you are given a carpet woven from the fleeces of a magical flock of sheep. This carpet has the ability to take you back to any period of history so you can walk the land, view the art, listen to the music, converse with the common people in their homes, and interview the most famous individuals of that time. Where would you tell your magic carpet to go? You could visit a medieval castle on the rocky coast of England, discuss philosophy with Socrates in the marketplace of Athens, ride with Billy the Kid and his gang, or even spend time with a great-great-great grandparent in their native land. We all have certain periods of history that fascinate us. We find we love to watch programs about the time and read books and articles that cover the period. It is interesting to ask ourselves, why did we choose this time and this place? Our fantasies and interests about a historical period can teach us much about what we value, treasure, and need to explore.

We are what we contemplate.

—Plato

THE MARCH OF TIME

Fellow citizens, we cannot escape history.
—Abraham Lincoln

What is the earliest major historical event you can remember? Was it Charles Lindbergh's historic flight across the Atlantic Ocean, the Great Depression, Pearl Harbor, the Korean War, or the assassination of John F. Kennedy? Our lives have spanned major events in the history of the world, and they have shaped the people we are today. People who weathered the Depression are probably amazed at the material goods that seem to be necessary to keep young people happy. Baby Boomers, who were activists in the sixties, may still feel the necessity of being deeply involved with the political process. We have all been shaped by the events that have flowed around our lives. Starting with your earliest memory, make a list of what you consider the major social, political, economic, and ideological events that have occurred in your lifetime. Your list might include anything from the introduction of Mickey and Minnie Mouse to the invention of the polio vaccine. When your list is complete, reflect on how your life would be different today if one of these events were removed from your history. This activity will show you how much you have been affected by events that have surrounded your life. This is an interesting activity to do with friends who are much younger than you. They will be fascinated by your stories, and you will also learn much about their world.

> *History is a child building a sandcastle by the sea, and that child is the whole majesty of man's power in the world.*
>
> —Heraclitus

MASKS

This is the closely guarded secret of life: that we are all caught up in a divine masquerade, and all we are trying to do is take off our masks to reveal the pure, perfect Self within.

—Eknath Easwaran

Many times in our lives we have retreated behind a mask. Our disguise may have been a scary Halloween mask, a gossamer wedding veil, or a painted clown's face. Humans have always created and worn masks. Paleolithic artists painted shamans in animal masks on cave walls, and archaeologists have uncovered funeral masks that are more than 5,000 years old. With the simple gesture of putting on a face that is not our own, we can undergo a transformation and become something totally different from what we are in our ordinary lives. We often hide behind non-material masks as well in order to protect our emotions and disguise our feelings. To be our authentic selves and go maskless is sometimes difficult, for then we become exposed and vulnerable. Opening ourselves to others and refusing to hide behind a mask can be a liberating and transforming experience.

It is best to be yourself, imperial, plain and true.

—Robert Browning

MAY DAY

Your way of giving is more important than what you give.

—Vietnamese Proverb

As more celebrations and events like Secretary's Day, Grandparents Day, and Super Bowl Sunday are added to our calendar, some older holidays are starting to disappear. For example, when was the last time you found a May basket sitting outside your front door? It is probably good that we eliminate a few special days, or we would become overwhelmed with all the greeting cards we had to purchase. It is sad, however, to see May Day lose its importance, for it goes a long way back into Western history. In early European times it was the day the Celts celebrated fertility, for they had just planted their fields and hoped for bounteous crops. At this time they would go into the woods and find the perfect tree to become the May Pole that was the center of the celebration. As children, we also honored the first of May by going into the countryside to collect wildflowers. After gathering the spring blossoms, we would fold, cut, and paste beautiful May baskets and make up the list of all the recipients. Not only friends received these surprises but also elderly neighbors. On the first day of May, we would creep silently to a front door, knock gently, and then quickly vanish down the street or sidewalk, giggling softly, happy and self-satisfied. Why not make May baskets this year and secretly leave them on your friends' doorsteps? The gift that is least expected is often the one that is most cherished.

Flowers leave some of their fragrance in the hand that bestows them.

—Chinese Proverb

MEMORABILIA

Memory is a net.

—Oliver Wendell Holmes

Year after year we accumulate more and more mementos. Many are gifts from treasured friends, inheritances from relatives, or souvenirs from our travels. A nice surprise is to discover a forgotten memento that has been tucked away for years: a ticket stub in an old purse, a twenty-year-old letter left inside a book, or even a grocery list that brings back memories of a special feast. As the years go by our walls, shelves, and closets become so crowded with these objects that we are forced to pack some away. It is hard, if not impossible, to part with some of these things, for when we look at them and touch them we can instantly recall special people and places. We almost need private archives for all these treasures so we can be near the things we hold so dear and that make up our material autobiography. What are your favorite mementos, and what memories do they bring back?

For where your treasure is, there will your heart be also.

—Matthew 6:21

MIRACLES

*There are two ways to live. One is as though nothing is a
miracle. The other is as though everything is.*

—Albert Einstein

If you ever lose faith in miracles, plant seeds in a small container, place
them by a sunny window, and then daily observe what is taking place.
In mid-winter it is also delightful to buy paperwhite narcissus bulbs,
set them in a bowl, and watch the gnarly bulbs crack open so that a
small sliver of green stalk can emerge, followed by fragrant, delicate
white blossoms. We live in an age of skepticism and doubt, and yet
miracles are swirling all around us. Not one day goes by without a
miracle transpiring in our lives. Today go out and look for one of
these. If you do not find one today, you can expect at least two tomorrow. Ask your friends about the miracles in their lives, and soon doubt
and skepticism about miracles will disappear.

*A miracle is an event that creates faith. That is the
purpose and nature of miracles.*

—George Bernard Shaw, *St. Joan*

MODERATION

Manifest plainness
Embrace simplicity
Reduce selfishnes
Have few desires.

—Lao Tzu

When is enough really enough? Look around your home, your community, and your country and see how many things are truly in excess. Throughout our lives we have filled our homes with too many knickknacks, our communities with too many cars and strip malls, and our country with too many weapons. We go to buffet brunches where it would be impossible for all the pastries and eggs benedict to be consumed by the diners. Our personal desires are also excessive—a closet full of clothes and shoes (have you ever counted them?); pantries bulging with canned goods; and entertainment centers overflowing with the latest technology. When we live with too many things, we live in a world of distractions, for we not only have to beep busy dusting, fixing, and operating all these possessions, but we also spend hours accumulating more. The task of simplifying is anything but simple, but it can be done. Start with one shelf, then a closet, then move to a room or maybe the garage. When a few individuals start the process of simplification, it may slowly move out to others until one day we find our community and even our nation choosing to live a more moderate lifestyle.

> *To be without some of the things you want is an indispensable part of happiness.*
>
> —Bertrand Russell

MONTHS

What are your most and least favorite months? Take all the months of
the year and rank them from one to twelve. Do you see a pattern in
your preferences? Do you seem to enjoy the cool months or the hot
months? Do you thrive during moist, dark, cloudy days or sunny days
with bright blue skies? We all have certain times of the year when we
feel at our best and others when we don't want to venture outside our
homes. Each of us has unique cycles, and we need to be aware of them
so that when we start feeling physical and emotional changes, we can
check to see whether they might have been brought about simply by
the time of year. There is not much we can do about the weather, but
we can brighten some of the darker days. If your favorite month is
April, find daffodils or tulips for the gray months of winter. If you love
the food of the October harvest, have apple cider and pumpkin pie in
February. We must relish the months that make us feel healthy and
full, and we must remember that the spark they bring into our lives
can be carried through the entire year.

THE MOON

I see the moon,
And the moon sees me.
God bless the moon,
And God bless me.

—Anonymous

Throughout the ages men and women have gazed at the moon and loved its mercurial nature. Because the moon takes on a new and mysterious appearance from phase to phase and from month to month, it has acquired many names: Harvest Moon, Blue Moon, Moon of the Red Grass Appearing, Green Corn Moon, Sturgeon Moon, Flower Moon, and on and on. The moon delights our senses, but it also causes great changes in our bodies. The moon can come within 218,000 miles of Earth, producing an incredible pull on the waters of the world. This same pull also affects the fluids in our own bodies, which is why we react to the phases of the moon. If you keep track of the moon's phases with a calendar or by going out and looking at the night sky, you will probably begin to understand how your body and spirit are tied to it. It is said that the eighth-century Chinese poet Li Po so loved the moon that one night he bent over in a boat to kiss its reflection, fell into the water, and drowned.

Sometimes I go about pitying myself. And all the while I am being carried across the sky.

—Ojibway Saying

MOTHER GOOSE

Ride a cock-horse
To Banbury Cross
To see a fine lady upon a white horse
Rings on her fingers and bells on her toes,
And she shall have music wherever she goes.

—Anonymous

Not many lovers of Mother Goose know that the fifteenth-century nursery rhyme "Ride a Cock-horse to Banbury Cross" is a poem describing the custom of wearing bells at the end of the tapering toe of a shoe. It was quite a fad, for it made clear to your neighbors that you were not a follower of Lucifer. And who would have thought that "Hey Diddle, Diddle the Cat and the Fiddle" had to do with the love between Queen Elizabeth I and Robert Dudley, Earl of Leicester? Almost every Mother Goose jingle we love has a historical root. Our beloved "Little Boy Blue" may actually have been Cardinal Wolsey of England, and "Humpty-Dumpty" was really an ale and brandy drink. "Miss Muffet" was Mary Queen of Scots, and the visiting spider was her longtime enemy, the Protestant reformer John Knox. As children we would not have wanted to know these fascinating facts, for we liked the sound of the rhyming, comforting words as they were read to us at bedtime. How many Mother Goose rhymes can you recall? It is fun to get a book of them and read them out loud. You will be surprised how many memories flood back. What was your favorite nursery rhyme? Why do you think you loved that one the most?

A truly great man never puts away the simplicity of a
child.

—Chinese Proverb

MOVEMENT

Butterfly never hurries even when pursued.
—Chinese Proverb

When we feel that we have reached a place of true stillness, it is hard to believe the world is moving at a rapid pace: cars speed on the highways; people frantically shop in the malls; our planet rotates on its axis at the rate of 1,000 miles an hour; and our hearts beat 4,320 times an hour, 103,680 times a day. Most of the time we are totally unaware of the cosmic dance going on around us. No matter how hard we might try, we cannot feel the speed of the earth's whirling or count all our heartbeats. It is enough to sit silently and be grateful for the forces that swirl around us and know there is always a "still point" where we can rest.

There is more to life than increasing its speed.
—Gandhi

THE MUSES

No great man has ever existed who had not some spark of divine inspiration.

—Cicero

The nine muses of ancient Greek mythology were the daughters of Zeus and Mnemosyne (memory). Their name is similar to *mens* in Latin and "mind" in English. They had the ability to bring to humans not only the forgetfulness of sorrows but also the power of memory. Today each of the nine is assigned an area of the arts and it is believed that just a light touch from one muse can ignite creativity in a human. Most of us hope that one day we will be the recipient of a creative spark that will allow us to achieve a longed-for accomplishment. We must, however, not wait any longer for this inspiring touch. We may not be able to achieve fame, much less fortune, but do we want to have passed through life and not given ourselves permission to try to express our creativity? What artistic endeavor have you always wanted to try? What is stopping you from exploring this right now in your life? Do not wait for an external muse but allow the internal one to break forth.

Perhaps our natural gifts elude us because they are so obvious.

—Sue Bender

MYTHS

Stories move in circles. They don't go in straight lines. So it helps to listen to them in circles. There are stories inside stories and stories between stories, and finding your way through them is as easy and as hard as finding your way home.

—Deena Metzger, quoting members of the
National Jewish Theater

Cultures use myths and fairy tales not only to entertain the young but also to instruct children in correct behavior and prepare them for the dangers and calamities that life can hold. *The Ugly Duckling, Hansel and Gretel,* and even *Peter Rabbit* have taught children that conflict is inevitable and that mistakes can be forgiven. These stories are timeless, and the ones that you loved as a small child are probably the same ones your children and grandchildren know by heart. What was your favorite childhood story or world myth? Who were your favorite heroes and/or heroines? Are these still your favorite tales? Why do you think these particular stories appealed to you? Do you still use their lessons in your life today?

Furthermore, we have not to risk the adventure alone, for the heroes of all time have gone before us.

—Joseph Campbell

NATURE'S SECRETS

If you break open the cherry tree,
Where are the blossoms?
But in Springtime
How they bloom!

—Ikkyu

Nature is filled with secrets and mysteries: an oak tree growing from the tiniest acorn; an elephant herd guarding the bones of their dead; a minute spider spinning an exquisite web. Humans try to dissect these mysteries in order to explain the unknown, for we are not comfortable with secrets. Nature, however, seems to enjoy keeping many of her mysteries unsolved. If we didn't continue to insist on unraveling all our planet's secrets, we could hold on to her many enchantments and thus could stand in continuous astonishment.

I don't pretend to understand the universe.

—Thomas Carlyle

OBLIGATIONS

We have the obligation to pass on the environment intact to the next generation. We are only brief sojourners on this planet and must consider what happens after we are gone.

—Fr. Thomas Keating

Often we are frustrated by the world our ancestors passed on to us. From our forebears we inherited all the mechanisms for total war and a world where nations feel compelled to compete with each other for economic and political power. They left us a world out of balance. We may complain about what we were given and forget to look at the world we are passing on. Our descendants are receiving from us diminishing rainforests and ozone layers, vanishing plant and animal species, and quantities of nuclear waste with no safe place to store them. Our world would be even more out of balance if there had not been men and women who spent their lives fighting for equality, endangered species, disarmament, and peace. We cannot personally fight each of these battles, but we must at least fight some. If everyone ignored the obligation we have, the next generation would have little to thank us for. We must take a realistic look at what is in the "estate" we will leave our heirs. Will they be safe? Will they feel protected? Will their world be beautiful and nurturing? We also need to be sure our descendants see their intergenerational obligation so that they too will guard and protect our planet.

Where you go, go with all your heart.

—Chinese Proverb

OBSTACLES

Life is a difficult task, for it seems we are always having to run an obstacle course filled with roadblocks, detours, and closure signs. The Hindu religion has a special god to take care of these hindrances. Ganesha, the destroyer of all obstacles, is the god of wisdom and knowledge. He is represented with the short, plump body of a man, the head of an elephant, and many hands holding auspicious symbols. All Hindu ceremonies start with an invocation to Ganesha, for he is the god one must first go to when starting a new adventure or undertaking. We all need encouragement when we begin something new or make our way through the maze of life's difficulties. The Hindu faith teaches us that it is useful to have a blessing and a companion in order to weather the obstacles that always seem to be in our way and on our path.

To succeed, keep on doing what it took to get started.
                                    —Anonymous

OOPS

Lord, keep my memory green.
—Charles Dickens

"Oops, did I turn off the coffee pot?" "Did I let the cat in?" "Did I really have a dental appointment today?" "I thought I opened the garage door!" We have years and years of duties, chores, and facts stored in our brains, and daily we must remember more and more. Many experts comfort us and say it is not that we are losing our memory—we simply have too much in storage and it gets scrambled, erased, or muddled. It is comforting when a partner or a friend seems to have the same problem, but it still does not do away with the frustrations and inconveniences memory lapses bring into our lives. We must face many new challenges each year, and the best thing we can do for ourselves is to keep our sense of humor when we have a "senior moment" or get "lazy in the brain."

With mirth and laughter let old wrinkles come.
—William Shakespeare

PANDORA'S BOX

Hope means hoping when everything is hopeless.

—G. K. Chesterton

As children we were delighted by the story of Pandora, the inquisitive young girl who was entrusted with a special box and told to "never, ever, open it." One day, Pandora could stand it no longer and lifted the lid. Out flew all the evils and illnesses of the world: greed, envy, sickness, and pain. She quickly closed the container, but it was too late; all the adversities that bring suffering into the world had escaped. Later she heard a small muffled voice coming from the box. "Let me out, let me out," it cried, and when she opened it, out flew hope. Humankind now had a way to deal with all its pain and suffering. When we are filled with discouragement and despair, it is hard to believe we will ever be able to experience happiness again. The ancient story of Pandora, however, reminds us that even though life brings suffering and pain, we are not abandoned because there will always be hope.

My hopes are not always realized but I hope.

—Ovid

PARADISE LOST

Though we travel the world over to find the beautiful, we must carry it with us or we find it not.

—Ralph Waldo Emerson

Our lives would be boring if we could not take imaginary journeys to mystical places like Shangri-La, Camelot, Avalon, or Atlantis. We do not know if these places actually existed, although archaeologists have excavated a hilltop in England that might have been King Arthur's home, and there is much speculation about the exact location of Atlantis. Many of us would like to keep these magical places imaginary so that we can have an "out of this world" travel experience. We now have the capability of traveling to any place on the globe: the source of the Nile, the top of Mt. Everest, and even the North and South Poles. Still, it is nice to think there are some places left unexplored, reserved for our wildest fantasies. If you could wander through the mystical geography of fiction and fantasy, where would you most like to visit? What could you learn from this mysterious trip? What difference could it make in your life?

Look and you will find.

—Sophocles

PARTNERS

There is no better mirror than a friend.
—Cape Verde Proverb

It is wonderful to meet new friends and begin new relationships, for it changes the nature of our lives and brings us new enjoyments. We never can replace, however, the old partners who have been through our many passages. These are the relationships that have withstood the test of time because we have loved each other through our impatience, anger, and even unforgiving hearts. When we share our history, moment by moment, with these special companions, they become the characters in the chapters of our lives. Building these deep partnerships takes time and commitment. We sometimes fail to tell our longtime friends how much they have meant to us and how much they have helped us grow. We are who we are today because of these individuals who have escorted us through the many stages of our lives.

Learning to love requires a lot of stamina and many years of hard work, and there is anguish in it as well as joy.
—Eknath Easwaran

PATIENCE

Patience is the companion of wisdom.

—St. Augustine

What is the situation that makes you the most impatient? Is it waiting in line at the grocery store? Being put on hold and not knowing when a person will come back on the line? Waiting at a stoplight? Waiting for a person who moves more slowly than you do? Impatience leads to inappropriate behavior and also inner turmoil. No one gains from impatient behavior. When you next feel impatience rising inside your body, distract yourself with something pleasing and pleasant: a poem, a song, or a peaceful place in your imagination. This will not only bring balance into your life but also prevent you from disrupting the lives of those around you.

Patience is bitter but its fruit sweet.

—Jean-Jacques Rousseau

PERCEPTION

We see what is behind our eyes.

—Chinese Proverb

Our brains determine exactly what our eyes see. For example, two individuals see broccoli in the grocery store, and one person's mouth waters with the thought of it swimming in a cheese sauce. The other sees a revolting green vegetable that was forced on them when they were young. The difference in the responses is caused not by the eyes of the shoppers but by their brains. Groups of people often suffer because of a culture's subjective "point of view." For example, in many parts of the world the elderly are the seat of wisdom and their experience is pivotal in major decision-making. In our culture, however, the wisdom of the elders is often not sought after or valued. It is not humanly possible to be totally objective, for our brains will always sort and sift, and we are influenced by our age, gender, and background. We can, however, be cautious and aware that our perception of another person or event can shut us off from experiences that would make us wiser and more compassionate.

If the doors of perception were cleansed everything in the world would appear to man as it is, infinite.

—William Blake

PETROGLYPHS

We all love to tell our own stories, and we appreciate anyone willing to take the time to listen to or read them. Our earliest ancestors also had a great need to pass on accounts of their lives and beliefs. Throughout the world we see these stories pecked and scratched on cave walls, stone outcroppings, and even large boulders. Archaeologists have not been able to decode all their meanings, but they believe the engravings are clan symbols, stories of hunts and migrations, genealogies—and some are simply graffiti. We love to find these ancient pictures of animals, shamans, and celestial bodies. To touch one immediately connects us to all these early ancestors. Even if we cannot be absolutely sure of the meaning of the glyphs, we know that hidden within the drawings and subtle marks are messages filled with knowledge and wisdom. We also tell our stories in order to pass on thoughts and experiences in the hope that they will entertain, enlighten, and guide others. Maybe hundreds of years from now our notes, letters, and journals will allow our descendants to understand our daily lives, our beliefs, and the events that shaped our world.

PILGRIMAGES

For in their hearts doth Nature stir them so,
Then people long on pilgrimage to go,
And palmers to be seeking foreign strands,
To distant shrines renowned in sundry lands.

—Geoffrey Chaucer, *The Canterbury Tales*

Our first thoughts when we think of pilgrims are the brave settlers who founded the colonies in the New World or the medieval travelers who joined together to travel to the cathedral at Canterbury. In our modern world, however, many people still make pilgrimages. A pilgrim, then or now, is on a quest and is pulled to a particular place in the hope that they will find answers to questions that have lingered in their minds for a long time. Many take religious pilgrimages to spiritual sites like Lourdres in France, the Wailing Wall in Jeruselum, Mount Kailish in Tibet, Mecca in Saudi Arabia, or Chaco Canyon in Arizona. Some pilgrims travel to sites where others have deeply suffered: Dachau, Wounded Knee, or Gettsyburg. Still others have as their destination a place that is special only to them: a grandparent's grave, the town where they were born, or the family homestead. These are all trips filled with reverence and curiosity, and when the pilgrim arrives at the destination they will know that they have completed an important personal quest.

Wherever you go, you will always bear yourself about
with you, and so you will always find yourself.

—Thomas à Kempis

PLANS

Let us spend one day as deliberately as Nature, and not be thrown off the track by every nutshell and mosquito's wing that falls on the rails.

—Henry David Thoreau

Is your calendar too full? Do you run out of time for things that nourish you? Do you become resentful when you have to leave the house to fulfill one more commitment? Being busy in our culture is a sign of success and is counted as an indicator of one's popularity, but it is not a way to bring peace and serenity into your life. We all need to be with people and also to be of service, but too much of our time is spent being "busy just to be busy." All of these commitments and appointments can be a distraction and prevent us from leading the lives we would really like to lead. You might want to start the process of simplifying your calendar by blocking off one day or one half day each week, just for you. When people call and ask that you become involved on that day, simply apologize and say the day is full. We know we deserve these hours; we are just not used to giving ourselves the time we are willing to give to others. How you use this time will be up to you, but try not to spend it filling up your calendar.

How beautiful it is to do nothing, and then rest afterward.

—Proverb

PLAYMATES

A true friend is one soul in two bodies.
—Aristotle

One of the most endearing circle of friends ever described is the one that played with Christopher Robin and lived in the Hundred-acre Wood. Who could have had more loyal playmates than Pooh, Rabbit, Tigger, Roo, Kanga, Owl, Eeyore, and Piglet? Each of these friends had faults and foibles, and yet the beauty of their circle was that they never judged or criticized each other. They risked their lives for their friends, went on endless treks to give assistance, and stayed at each other's sides through thick and thin. Their friendship was rock-solid, and that is probably why people of all ages are drawn to their stories. We all wish our own friendships could be so unconditional. Trust is built when we know we are not going to be judged unfairly. Loyalty develops over years of knowing that a friend will always be available to help in any way. When we make our friends a priority in our lives and commit ourselves to their health and growth, we will gather around us a circle of friends as loving as the playmates in the Hundred-acre Wood.

Hold a friend with both hands.
—Nigerian Proverb

POSTCARDS

A friend is a poem.

—Persian Proverb

It is satisfying and comforting to send postcards from faraway places to family and friends. When you write from an outdoor café in Paris, the rim of the Grand Canyon, or the steps of a temple in Kathmandu, you are telling your friends that at that exact moment, in that exotic place, you are holding them in your thoughts. Postcards leave little room for news about your travels, so all they can convey is the message that even though you are surrounded by marvelous distractions, miles from home, you need to let them know you are thinking of them. One does not have to be in a foreign place to send a short message on a postcard. You can buy postcards of the sites in your own city or town, print the date and exact time you were thinking of your friend, and then let the message sweep across the miles.

Two souls and one thought, two hearts and one pulse.

—Halen

POTENTIAL

We seldom respect ourselves enough.

—Plautus

As we grow older and realize that our physical capabilities are declining, many of us mistakenly make an assumption that our non-physical potential is also decreasing. This is not true. We do not lose our capacity for inner growth just because we no longer can run a marathon or surf dangerous ocean waves. In fact, with age our potentials can increase and allow us to move into different fields. The increase in our potential is due to a lifetime of experiences, which has brought us wisdom and knowledge and the capability to succeed in new areas. The first step is to recognize what these talents and capabilities are. We must examine ourselves and achieve what Socrates proclaimed was the most important task for any man or woman: "Know thyself."

I do not want to die . . . until I have faithfully made the most of my talent and cultivated the seed that was placed in me until the last small twig has grown.

—Kathe Kollwitz

A POT OF GOLD

Only the heart knows how to find what is precious.

—Fyodor Dostoyevsky

Many of us make wishes on stars, wishbones, and rainbows because we believe wishes come true. Try this imaginary journey and you may discover an unfulfilled wish you didn't know you had.

Imagine that after an afternoon rain you find the beginning of a rainbow bridge and you follow the colorful arch upward. At the top you can see the horizon encircling you. As you start down the rainbow path your eyes catch the glimmer of a tiny golden pot dripping with raindrops and glistening in the sun. As you get closer you see that it has a golden lid. You kneel down, slowly lift the lid, and peak inside. What is waiting inside that is just for you?

> *There wouldn't be such a thing as counterfeit gold if there were no real gold somewhere.*
>
> —Sufi Proverb

POWERS OF THE MIND

Our society promotes cleverness instead of wisdom, and celebrates the most superficial, harsh and least useful aspects of our intelligence.

—Sogyal Rinpoche

If you had your choice, which of the following would you be?

(a) Knowledgeable
(b) Intelligent
(c) Wise

There are big differences among these three choices. We are born with intelligence; we can acquire knowledge by reading and studying; wisdom comes only over time with patience, courage, reflection, and love. We live in a culture that admires intelligent entrepreneurs and knowledgeable scholars. It is often believed that the ones with wisdom lived at a different time as philosophers or mystics who meditated on lonely mountaintops. We all, however, have been given the capacity for wisdom, regardless of our innate intelligence or the amount of knowledge we have amassed. If we open ourselves to love, become more accepting of others, and think with our hearts, we will become wisdom-keepers for the world.

As irrigators lead water where they want, as archers make their arrows straight, as carpenters carve wood, the wise shape their minds.

—The Buddha

PREJUDICES

*I tell you one thing, if you want peace of mind do not
find fault with others. Rather learn from your own faults.*

—Sarada Devi

Prejudice is based on ignorance and fear. It occurs when one group believes its power, wealth, contentment, and status are being threatened. One way some groups solve this dilemma is by putting distance between themselves and the feared group. Ethnic minorities, women, and senior citizens have been the victims of this form of discrimination, and they have often been made invisible because of it. Anthropologists know that one way cultures can punish those who refuse to fit into the norm is by ostracizing them. This means the community will not acknowledge in any meaningful way that these people exist, even though they are allowed to remain living with the group. Prejudice often leads to this same form of discrimination, and as we grow older we may feel that we have become invisible to others in our society. We must all be on our guard against any prejudice that would allow another human being to effectively disappear from sight. Throughout the day check your behavior and honor every human being you meet with loving recognition.

*Prejudices are our robbers; they rob us of valuable things
in life.*

—Anonymous

PRIORITIES

One never notices what has been done; one can only see what remains to be done.

—Marie Curie

When our to-do list gets longer and longer, we sometimes lose perspective on what really needs to be done. It seems mindboggling to tackle the quantity of tasks on our list, and often we fail to do any of them. Other times, simply getting started seems so overwhelming that we start at the top and work our way down instead of prioritizing. Unfortunately, however, the first "to dos" are often the ones that could be put off for days or even weeks. It takes extra time to set clear priorities, but we need to slowly and carefully sort and sift through the demands and determine what truly must be done. It is also important to remember that the world will not stop if the tasks are not completed. As you work on your list you may discover that what is most important is not even on your list: a leisurely breakfast, a call to a friend, or taking the dog for an early morning walk.

Besides the noble art of getting things done, there is the noble art of leaving things undone. The wisdom of life consists in the elimination of the nonessential.

—Lin Yutang

PURPOSE OF LIFE

A really great talent finds its happiness in execution.

—Goethe

Each and every person who has ever lived or is now living on this planet has been and is unique from all others. Each has been given a different combination of eyes, smiles, height, and talents. All have housed within them different potentials and distinctive ways to express themselves. The purpose of our life is to find these special gifts and share them with the rest of humanity. Some people will become famous because of their ability to create musical or literary master-pieces, and others will play a part on the world's political stage. Many will choose a less public forum and become clerks, nurse's aids, teach-ers, farmers, and healers. Our contributions and the way we serve others will also change as we move through life, and so we must con-tinually ask ourselves the questions: What are my gifts and attributes at this time in my life? How can I best use them to bring happiness into my life and into the lives of others?

The power of a man's virtues should not be measured by
his special efforts, but by his ordinary doing.

—Pascal

PUSSY WILLOWS

What a pity flowers can utter no sound. A singing rose, a whispering violet, a murmuring honeysuckle—oh, what a rare and exquisite miracle would these be!

—Henry Ward Beecher

When spring arrives with the first crocuses, daffodils, and tulips, it is hard to remember the last rose of summer that slowly succumbed to the first chilly fall evenings. Spring has finally come, and we rejoice with these harbingers of the season. Soon, however, these early spring blooms disappear and summer daisies, columbines, and phlox take over. Spring is gone, all except the pussy willows that we clipped just when they were at their furry best. These gifts of spring are such a blessing, for they promise to remind us of the spring of their birth, not only through the coming summer, fall, and winter, but for many seasons to come. Pussy willows have "staying power"; they are not fair-weather friends. We are blessed with a few friends who are like pussy willows. They are the ones who know the history of each of our seasons and will be around for many more to come.

Love from one being to another can only be that two solitudes come nearer, recognize and protect and comfort each other.

—Han Suyin

PUZZLES

One must still have chaos in one to give birth to a dancing star.

—Nietzsche

There are times in our lives when we feel as if we are a 1,000-piece jigsaw puzzle that we have been working on for a long time and making substantial progress. Then all of a sudden, fate dumps the puzzle on the floor, and only a few pieces remain joined together. Our lives can become a jumble in a wink of an eye. We are going along successfully piecing it together, and then in one second our life appears to be in shambles. The only thing that can really be done during these times is to start slowly working on the puzzle. Turning over the pieces and sorting them helps us take a few deep breaths, and it also keeps us engaged in what must be done. We must also not forget to look for guidance from others just as we get help by looking at the picture on the top of the box. The process takes patience and determination, but we have no choice: it is our life and it cannot remain in fragments.

To succeed, keep on doing what it took to get started.

—Anonymous

QUESTIONS

I want to live in the question. Answers tend to close things off.

—Fr. M. Basil Pennington

Young children and those in the second half of their lives seem to be the ones who ask questions that do not have easy answers or even one correct answer. As children, we ask question in order to gain knowledge about our world and our place within the universe: How far away are the stars? When can I have a real bicycle? Is there a heaven? As we age we ask questions from a need to know more details about the heart and soul: What gives me hope? How can I become more loving? What is the purpose of my life? When we ask these questions we should not try to arrive at an answer too quickly, for the process allows us to explore ourselves. Sometimes questions about our legacy and destiny seem so difficult that we want to skirt around them or put them on hold. This delaying tactic means only that they will reappear in other, perhaps more urgent or unsettling, forms. By welcoming questions that well up from the heart and soul, we allow ourselves to go on an inward journey. This pilgrimage will allow us to grow and transform.

When a question is posed ceremoniously the universe responds.

—Chinese Proverb

QUILTS

The quilts spoke to such a deep place inside me that I felt them reaching out. . . . How can a quilt be calm and intense at the same time?

—Sue Bender

Of the many heirlooms passed from one generation to the next, the quilt is often the most cherished. Descendants often prefer a quilt to a grandmother's silver or an aunt's china. Maybe this is because we can wrap this treasured piece of the past around ourselves and feel not just cozy, but protected by our lineage. A quilt was a work in progress for many months, if not years. Shapes were cut, pieced together like a jigsaw puzzle, painstakingly stitched together, and then quilted into a complex whole. As our fingers trace the patterns created by thousands of tiny stitches, we realize that a quilt is a perfect metaphor for our lives. We are also a complex work of many pieces that has slowly come together, and through time the scraps were stitched into a wondrous and beautiful whole. Perhaps our good deeds and contributions will be as lasting as a quilt that is gently and carefully passed from one generation to the next.

Do you realize or understand your own nobility?

—St. Macarius

REGRETS

To err is human.

—Alexander Pope

It is important to be able to separate big regrets from small regrets. We may feel sorry that we forgot to send a friend a birthday card or call a family member to say "hello." These regrets will pass and soon be forgotten. Then we have the regrets we cannot easily erase from our minds, and as we grow older, this collection seems to grow larger. Some of these can be corrected if we are brave and forthright and are willing to make amends to those whom we have hurt. Sometimes, however, it is not possible because the person we injured is no longer available to accept our apology. It is not wise to let mistakes take up a permanent home inside of us. We do need, however, to remember the cause of our mistake so that we can prevent ourselves from making the same error again. Then it is time to move on, knowing that it is possible that our deep regret is an apology in itself.

When God wishes a man well, he gives him insight into his own faults.

—Muslim Proverb

RELATIONSHIPS

You learn to speak by speaking, to study by studying, to run by running, to work by working; in just the same way, you learn to love by loving.

—St. Francis de Sales

When you think back on the most significant relationships in your life, you will immediately remember the time, commitment, and dedication necessary to maintain them and allow them to grow. There is great joy in building a partnership, but there is nothing easy about learning how to live with patience and forgiveness. Both members in a relationship must have "staying power," for acts are committed that make one partner or the other want to retreat or even give up. When the storm has been weathered, however, and the relationship tested, the bond is stronger than could ever have been expected. It is hard to love without conditions, but when we have fewer and fewer demands and expectations, a partnership can be forged that nothing will be able to break.

My bounty is as boundless as the sea,
My love as deep, the more I give to thee
The more I have, for both are infinite.

—William Shakespeare, *Romeo and Juliet*

RESILIENCY

Be not afraid of growing slowly, be afraid of only standing still.

—Chinese Proverb

Resiliency is the ability to bounce back, to bend and not break, to be stretched to our limit and still not give up. In our lives we have all been in situations where we felt we had been pushed to the extreme and we could not take anymore. At that time, however, a force inside of us most likely came to our rescue, and we continued to move through what we had thought was truly an impossible situation. We are more resilient than we can imagine. We all have the ability to bend and bounce back, no matter how weary and discouraged we might feel. Resiliency is a gift we have all been given, and it is our job to remember the flexible strength within us.

"I'm very brave generally," he went one in a low voice, "only today I have a headache."

—Lewis Carroll, *Tweedledum*

RESPECT

Kindness begets kindness.

—Sophocles

How do you want to be treated by others? Do you treat others that way? Do you pay attention to the person checking out your groceries? Do you return phone calls? Do you keep other people waiting? Do you fail to return a friendly hello as you walk down a corridor or sidewalk? We sometimes become so self-absorbed that we fail to treat those around us with respect. These failed connections or responses may indicate to the other person that you feel your time is more precious than theirs or that you do not feel they are worthy of your regard. This is probably not what you intended, but when we become totally involved in our own problems and our own lives, we become neglectful of those we encounter throughout the day. It takes time and thought to treat those around us as we wish to be treated.

What you do speaks so loudly, I cannot hear what you say.
—Ralph Waldo Emerson

RETREAT

I want to go soon and live by the pond, where I shall hear only the wind whispering among the reeds. It will be a success if I shall have left myself behind. But my friends ask what I will do when I get there. Will it not be employment enough to watch the progress of the seasons?

—Henry David Thoreau

Sometimes the world is too much with us and we need to take a break. As small children, when we had that feeling we would threaten to "run away from home." As adults we continue to have these feelings. It is not that we do not love the people and things that surround us; we simply need time to be by ourselves to think, ponder, or puzzle about the meaning of our life and the direction we want to move. It is sometimes logistically difficult to have a week alone on the beach or even a weekend in a quiet retreat center. We can, however, take a day or even half a day and go to a nearby park or even retreat into a quiet corner of our home. We need to explain to the people close to us what we are doing so they can help us find a period of peace and quiet. This is not a luxury. This is an essential part of living. Being by ourselves in silence and solitude is a way to find our way back home.

Even silence speaks.

—Danish Proverb

RISKS

Taking a new step, uttering a new word is what people fear most.

—Fyodor Dostoyevsky

What are some things you have always wanted and planned to do but have never done? Some may have required more time than you had or more money than you earned. Others may have been within your resources, but you didn't do them because you were too timid or afraid that you might fail. Which of these adventures are you still thinking about today? Which are still within your means and physical capabilities? There are many ways we can fulfill these dreams. If you always wanted to take gymnastic classes, now you could try yoga. If you always wanted to scuba dive, you could now learn to snorkel. There are so many things within our grasp: taking an art class, writing poetry, learning how to explore the Internet, taking part in an archaeological dig. Satisfying our desires is a way to be happy and feel complete. If we don't try these adventures now, when will we?

While we are postponing, life speeds by.

—Seneca

ROOTS

Roots nourish, give us life, and bind us safely to earth.
Plant them well.

—Anonymous

The way we pick up and move around the country, or even the globe, is a bit like playing musical chairs. A signal is given; we pack up, follow a moving van, and settle in a new place. Living in many different areas of the country or the world gives us new perspectives, but it doesn't give our roots a chance to sink deeply into the ground. When we find ourselves moving to a new home, it is important to stay connected to the special people we leave behind. During these times we may feel rootless, so it is important to remember that family and friends can continue to be our support system and dispel the loneliness we might feel.

Our lives are like islands in the sea, or like trees in
the forest, which co-mingle their roots in the darkness
underground.

—William James

RUINS

When we have the opportunity to walk through ancient archaeological sites, we often feel the presence of those who once called the place their home. The roofs of their dwellings have disappeared, their homes are mounds of dirt, and their places of worship are empty—or are they? Sometimes when we stand inside their kivas, temples, churches, or stupas, we can feel the energy and power of the ceremonies and rituals that took place in these sacred places. If we listen carefully we can almost hear the drums, cymbals, songs, and chants of the people. We are drawn to these places: Stonehenge, Ankgor Wat, the Pyramids, the catacombs of Rome, and Machu Picchu. When we visit these ancient sites, we come with the hope that we might hear the spirits of the ancients whispering truths in our ear. These people were exactly like us: they worked hard, raised families, laughed and told jokes, had conflicts with other groups, and worshiped a god or gods that protected and nourished them. Someday our homes, schools, and places of worship will also be buried deep within the ground, and visitors may come back and wander our streets and wonder what kind of folks called this place home.

SANCTUARY

Heaven is under our feet as well as over our heads.
—Henry David Thoreau

From Paleolithic to modern times, humans have constructed sacred spaces. These ancient places can be found deep within caves, inside a circle of monolithic stones, or on top of mounds of earth that have been molded into the shapes of birds and beasts. Today we find spiritual homes inside churches, temples, synagogues, mosques, and any place where humans gather and say, "This is our most holy space." When we enter a prehistoric sanctuary, we can only guess what rites and rituals took place there, but we know that the spot marked the place that separated the sacred from the mundane. It also was a space where people could seek protection from outside forces. We all need a safe place that removes us from the ordinary world. Some of us can find this within our community of friends, and others in a religious congregation. We also can create sanctuaries in our homes and even in our minds; it just needs to be the place that is filled with peace and moves us to a higher level of consciousness.

You have to believe in gods to see them.
—Hopi Saying

SCARS

We are healed by our suffering only by experiencing it to the full.

—Marcel Proust

When we take an inventory of all the scars that mark our bodies, we can practically use them as an outline for an autobiography. Some are so tiny and invisible that they are hard to find or even remember. Others are still vivid, and it seems like only yesterday when we fell from a certain tree or a bike. Unfortunately, scars are not just a childhood occurrence, for as we age we add new ones that remain raw and tender to the touch. We have within us as many scars as appear on the outsides of our bodies. These come from rejections, separations, and losses and are the hardest ones to heal. We can learn about hope from all our scars, for after the suffering and tears have passed all that will remain is a small reminder of the wound. Take a look at your scars. Can you place a date on each one? Can you remember the lessons it taught you?

Troubles are often the tools by which God fashions us for better things.

—Henry Ward Beecher

SEEDS

The entire universe is concentrated in a garden.

—Sabin Yamada

The next time you open a seed packet, pick out one tiny seed and imagine that you can see within it the flower or plant it will become. How is it possible that this tiniest of containers holds within it a stalk of celery, a bright late-summer zinnia, or even an enormous watermelon? It is amazing to think that when we eat seeds and nuts, we are taking into ourselves walnut trees, sunflowers, pumpkins, and all the energy needed for their growth. What a miracle that all the creatures of nature originate from the tiniest seeds, nuts, and eggs. How often do you think about these wonders of nature and remember to give thanks?

The seed never explains the flower.

—Edith Hamilton

SEEING

I shut my eyes in order to see.

—Paul Gauguin

Seeing takes a great deal of concentration and time. We move through our world glancing this way and that, quickly looking at traffic lights, bits of dust on a table, or multitudes of packaged goods on grocery shelves. We look, but we do not see. Seeing takes a conscious effort to slow down and allow your gaze to be fixed on an object. Take time to see a flower; look closely at the tiny particles of pollen dust, the change of color on each petal, the exact tiny place where the leaf sprouts from the stem. Look at those around you in the same manner. The word *seer* means a person with a depth of wisdom and foresight. We can also become seers if we take time to look deeply and closely at our world. When we do we will find new universes in the eyes of a friend and in one single leaf of a tree.

For the outer sense alone perceives visible things and the eye of the heart alone sees the invisible.

—Richard of Saint-Victor

SELF–FULFILLING

PROPHESIES

Monday's child is fair of face,
Tuesday's child is full of grace,
Wednesday's child is full of woe,
Thursday's child has far to go,
Friday's child is loving and giving,
Saturday's child works hard for his living,
But the child that is born on the Sabbath day
Is blithe and bonny, and good and gay.
— A. B. Bray, *Traditions of Devonshire*

When we were young children, our parents would tell us that we were smart, hesitant, too thin-skinned, impatient, or cute. We often accepted the labels our relatives gave us before we had a chance to understand the significance of our attributes. When we went off to school, teachers added more: "She is a math genius"; "He will never be able to sing"; "She should grow up and be a nurse." Many times we added to these imposed attributes by telling ourselves, "I am too shy and will never be able speak in public," or "My eyes are too small; how can I ever be considered a beauty?" Unfortunately, we have allowed ourselves to grow into some of these false descriptors, and no matter how beautiful we have become or how articulate we are, we have clung to these past characterizations. It is never too late to take an objective look at ourselves and discard these inaccurate assessments so that we can recognize the person we really are.

Know thyself.
— Inscription found on the Temple to Apollo, Delphi, Greece

SENIORS

Be content with the strength you've got.
—Spanish Proverb

When we were young, to be a senior meant that we were the oldest and wisest in our high schools and thus had certain rights and privileges, which often included keeping the freshmen in their place. Today the American Association of Retired Persons has given being a senior new meaning, for at the young age of fifty we are given a card that allows us to get into places of entertainment at a discount and to get bargains on certain days in shopping malls. The arrival of this card is normally met with shock, for it seems like only yesterday we were high school seniors with diplomas in hand, ready to conquer the world. Now that we have once again earned this title, a new set of challenges awaits us. At this stage in our lives, however, we are better prepared to face the new adventures, for we are more capable of mixing youthful idealism with mature realism.

Age only matters when one is aging. Now that I have arrived at a great age, I might as well be twenty.
—Pablo Picasso

SILENCE

True silence is the rest of the mind; it is to the spirit what sleep is to the body and nourishment to the soul.

—William Penn

How many minutes a day do you allow yourself to sit in silence? It is often hard to find a place or a time, but it is perhaps one of the most nourishing and essential things we can do for ourselves. Silence allows us to go inward more deeply than any other activity that fills our busy days. It is wise to explain to those close to us what we are doing; when they see our commitment to having a moment of peace and quiet, they might be called to follow our example.

Silence is the true friend that never betrays.

—Confucius

SKIPPING STONES

Observe the wonders as they occur around you. Don't claim them. Feel the artistry moving through, and be silent.

—Rumi

How good were you as a child at skipping stones? No matter how hard we tried, we never could do it quite as well as the adults. Maybe it was the size of their hands or even their height, but they always seemed to be master skippers. After they selected a perfectly round, flat stone, they would gently curl index finger and thumb around it, throw their arm out to the side, and release the stone . . . then . . . *skip, skip, skip, skip, plunk,* and it was gone. We would then wait and watch the second act, which was seeing the surface of the water fill with concentric circles growing, touching, and finally merging into each other. Each skip created its own circle that quickly reached out to embrace the next. When we watched this with our young eyes, we had no idea that the pattern of interconnecting circles was an image of what our life would soon become. One event followed by another and another, but all reaching out and connecting and holding each other's edges. Each milestone in our life is like one skip of a stone separated from the next and yet entwined, creating the whirling, growing pattern of our life.

The world is round and the place which may be the end may also be the beginning.

—Ivy Baker Priest

SLOWING DOWN

Life is so short we must move very slowly.
—Thai Saying

One of the hazards of modern living is always being in a hurry and being surrounded by other people who are also in a rush. This begins the moment we throw back our covers in the morning and have our first cup of coffee. We often start bustling around, not because we have that much to do but because it is a habit we have developed and our bodies seem to have gotten used to a particular speed. The acceptable miles per hour at which we are accustomed to operating can be changed if we become conscious of the fact that we are speeding up. We can miss out on our life if we hurry through it. It takes time to see the beautiful faces of loved ones or the color of the flowers we have planted with such care. "Hurry sickness" not only shortens our lives, but it also robs them of their true meaning.

Make haste slowly.
—Augustus Caesar

SNOWBOUND

There is no such thing as bad weather.

—John Ruskin

Weather has a way of giving us a vacation when we least expect it. Inches of snow piling up outside the door or a pelting rain, fog, or mist can give us an excuse to take the day off. As children we waited for school to be canceled because we then became absolutely liberated: no homework, no tests, no lectures. It is advantageous if our bad weather arrives on a weekend or a day when appointments can be canceled, for then we can stay at home without worries and decide what to do with twenty-four unstructured hours. There are times, however, when we are in need of a snow day, but the weather is perfect—and so we feel we must be "up and about." On one of these days, check your schedule and see if you can create your own bad-weather day. If it is possible, cancel your appointments, make a pot of tea, check the shelves for the book you have been wanting to read, and give yourself freedom to retreat into a cozy period of relaxation.

Better to idle well than to work badly.

—Spanish Proverb

SOLSTICES

Overcome the earth and the stars will be yours.

—Boethius

Some of the most inventive and creative structures of the world were built with the purpose of alerting our ancient ancestors to the approaching summer and winter solstices. In early winter the ancients saw the sun getting lower and lower and feared it might disappear below the horizon forever. During this time of increasing darkness the Egyptians honored the death and entombment of Osirus, and the Romans blended the nativities of Mithra, Apollo, Horus, and Theseus. As the sun inched higher and higher into the sky and reached the summer solstice, celebrations for fertility took place throughout the world. Today we have so many other celebrations on our calendars that we rarely remember these two auspicious dates. What natural event, however, is more important than the cycle of the sun, for our entire existence depends on this bright star. A celebration of the sun can be as simple as watching, with gratitude, its solstice rising and setting and remembering to do the same in years to come.

Accuse not nature, she hath done her part; Do thou but thine.

—John Milton

SOUNDS

There is no way in which to understand the world without first detecting it through the radar net of our senses.

—Diane Ackerman

What is your favorite sound? Is it the wind rustling leaves outside your window, a purring cat, the song of a mourning dove, or a pipe organ playing Bach? Sometimes when we least expect it we hear our favorite sound and it forces us to stop and rest within its voice or note. Some of our favorite sounds are disappearing. It is hard to hear the sound of a train rattling on its tracks, church and school bells, or the song of birds, because traffic and other modern noises are covering up their sweet sounds. As some of our favorite sounds vanish from our lives, we have to reach out and find new ones to take their place, for a special sound can hold us in a moment and make time stand still.

Listen from within.

—Thomas Edison

SOUVENIRS

But I always think the best way to love God is to love many things.

—Vincent Van Gogh

Souvenirs fill the nooks and crannies of our homes. Many of these treasures are mementos from our travels, keepsakes from our childhood, or gifts from loved ones. Most likely, many of these objects have been in the same place for so many years that we fail to notice them. We dust around them but rarely spend time with each one and allow it to take us back to a favorite place or memory. When others look at our souvenir collection they cannot know all the secrets and memories contained within each one, nor can they understand that each is a part of a chapter of our life. Spend time with these souvenirs, for there is a good reason why you have kept them for so many years.

Teach us to delight in simple things.

—Rudyard Kipling

SPONTANEITY

How often is happiness destroyed by preparation, foolish preparation?

—Jane Austen

As we get older it seems we lose the ability to react to new situations in a spontaneous way. Years of experience and responsibilities have taught us the skills of planning and the benefits of efficient organization. These are worthwhile human attributes, but we also need to have the self-discipline to set them aside and risk becoming spontaneously involved in new and enriching experiences. Habits and comfortable routines often dictate what we allow ourselves to do. We must, however, give ourselves permission to try new things and take exciting risks. Certainly we do not want to spend our lives moving erratically from one unplanned activity to the next, but we must learn to "unplan" our lives so we can more deeply participate in life.

Life was meant to be lived, and curiosity must be kept alive. One must never, for whatever reason, turn his back to life.

—Eleanor Roosevelt

SPRING CLEANING

Don't worry, spiders,
I keep house
Casually.

—Issa

One chore most of us dread and would like to hire others to do for us is spring housecleaning. A long time ago, one of our ancestors started this tradition by decreeing that in the spring every inch of a house should be cleaned and aired, whether it needed it or not. How we accomplished this onerous task often became proof of our housekeeping skills and abilities. How sad that spring was the chosen season for this chore, for in the months of May and June the world is bursting forth in bloom, and parks, gardens, and secret haunts are calling us. When spring comes we must decide between spring housecleaning or sitting in the warmth of a fresh spring day. We must ask ourselves what is the most important thing to do—air the curtains, wash the windows, and turn the mattresses or greet the world just as it awakes from its long winter sleep.

Consider that this day will never dawn again.

—Dante

STAGES OF LIFE

The fatal metaphor of progress, which means leaving
something behind us, has utterly obscured the idea of
growth, which means leaving something inside us.

—G. K. Chesterton

In Hindu cultures, life is divided into four stages, each with special tasks and responsibilities. The first stage is that of student, which is the time when knowledge and skills are acquired. This leads to the second stage of householder, which is when a profession is pursued and a family established. The second half of life also has two stages. The first of these is that of retirement. At this time, when the children take over the household duties, the older person can pursue a life away from the responsibilities of job and family. This is a time to reflect on the meaning of life, which leads to the last stage—that of renunciation. Each of these stages has a definite goal: first the acquisition of knowledge that leads to the active life of family and job, and then on to a life devoted to reflection and spirituality. In our culture we divide life into youth, middle age, and old age, and we also see definite goals attached to each. In youth we receive our education, in middle age we work for prosperity for our family and ourselves, and in old age we hope for an enjoyable retirement and a secure and safe old age. Our culture does not address the spiritual search the Hindus feel is the essential part of the last half of life. However, during the second half of life many of us become more searching and reflective, and this inward movement makes this stage one of great happiness and quiet joy.

Life is a succession of lessons which must be lived to be
understood.

—Helen Keller

STANDING STILL

Sit quietly, doing nothing, spring comes and the grass grows by itself.

—Zen Saying

When you were a child, did you play the game of "Statue"? The rules were simple: One person would whirl each player around and around, and when they were released they would pose absolutely frozen in the moment. The point was to see which player could be the most "statue-like" and stay immobile the longest. What if for three minutes, everything in the world came to a screeching halt and grew absolutely still, just like in the game of "Statue"? Traffic lights would stop, trains would halt, wars would cease, and all power would be turned off for 180 seconds. What could we learn from this "standing still"? Would those seconds teach us to slow down and pay more attention to others, or would we shrug and move on without learning anything? The inhabitants of Taos Pueblo in New Mexico have a period they call "Time for Staying Still." It is the time after the crops are harvested and before the winter settles in. This is the time between two seasons that speaks of birth and death. The inhabitants of the pueblo are provided this "still time" to think about the meaning of their lives and the lives of those around them. What could you learn in your life if you had a "Time for Staying Still"? What changes would it bring into your life?

Now my soul has elbow room.

—William Shakespeare

STAR DUST

Everything has its wonders, even darkness and silence, and I learn whatever state I may be in there to be content.

—Helen Keller

There is a certain amount of comfort in knowing that we go through the same life stages as a star. Stars have an explosive birth and a lusty youth and then collapse at the time of death. These life cycles last between six to eleven billion years. Stars are born in a nebula, which is a star nursery. At their conception huge clouds of dust and gas collapse under gravitational force, which produces a protostar that further collapses and produces a star as we know it. It then begins its youth, filled with astonishing energy, for it has jets trillions of miles long and can travel at speeds up to 500,000 miles an hour—an adolescent burst our teenagers can envy. As stars grow older they expand even more and produce more stellar wind than their younger version. The bigger stars actually have a shorter life because they burn such massive amounts of nuclear fuel. As age catches up with them their color changes and they explode, collapse, and become black dwarfs, neutron stars, or even black holes. How wondrous that all things in nature have a natural cycle, and how comforting it is to know that the passage from birth to death, from creation to destruction, is one that we share with our favorite star. Some night when you are in need of advice about the aging process, go out and look at a star and let it help you on this path.

Even a small star shines in the darkness.

—Danish Proverb

STARS

All men have the stars . . . but they are not the same things for different people. For some, who are travelers, they are guides. For others they are no more than lights in the sky. You—you alone—have the stars as no one else has them.

—Antoine de Saint-Exupéry

Every year our stars seem more distant as the bright lights of our cities and our careless pollution diminish their bright, golden glow. The night sky has changed little over the course of time, but if we want to view the intensity of the sky as our great-great-grandparents did, we must go far from urban areas. When we can see the stars so clearly, our hearts almost stop at the beauty and magnitude of their brilliance. Stars could make us feel inconsequential, but instead they allow us to feel part of a greater whole.

The toe of a star-gazer is often stubbed.

—Russian Proverb

STEPPING STONES

The true art of memory is attention.
—Samuel Adams

We have all hiked to a stream or creek and wondered where we would be able to cross safely. If we were lucky, we found a place where nature or man had placed stepping stones across the water that would allow us to reach the other side. Our lives are made of many such stepping stones—crucial moments, both painful and joyful, that shaped the people we are today and took us to new levels of understanding. Go back and recall the crucial stones that made all the difference, the ones that allowed you to keep your balance and pointed you in the right direction. When you think about these events, you know that if someone had removed one stone you might not have made a safe crossing. In your mind's eye, view this rocky path across the stream of your life and write one word on each stepping stone as a reminder of the events that brought you where you are today.

Memory is the cabinet of imagination.
—Basile

SURVIVAL

Man is harder than rocks and more fragile than an egg.

—Yugoslav Proverb

Our prehistoric ancestors lived in a precarious world, continuously threatened by the elements and ferocious beasts. Experts are sure, however, that there were not many type A personalities or people who suffered stress-related illnesses. Their advantage was that when a threat entered their lives (a mountain lion outside their cave), they had two options: they could fight it or run away. "Fight or flight" released adrenaline in their bodies, and when the stress passed, their bodies could quickly return to normal. Today, unfortunately, we often do not have the freedom to fight or flee. When we are faced with the threat of losing a job, being sued, or getting a traffic ticket, we cannot either beat up the other party or run away. Adrenaline, therefore, keeps coursing through our bodies, which can often lead to stress-related illnesses. In stressful situations, one small but important thing we can do is to breathe deeply. Under stress, our breathing becomes shallow and this is the exact moment when we need extra oxygen. So when stress enters your life, remember that it not only affects your emotions but also your physical well-being.

> *When you get into a tight place and everything goes against you, till it seems as though you could not hang on a minute longer, never give up then, for that is just the place and the time the tide will turn.*
>
> —Harriet Beecher Stowe

SYNCHRONICITY

Nothing is as it appears.

—The Buddha

It is always a shock to reach for the phone to call a friend only to have the phone ring at just that moment, and there she is on the line. Our lives are filled with coincidences like this, but we have also experienced coincidences beyond probability. Let's say that same friend is calling to say she read an amazing quote in a new book and wants to share it with you. *How can this be?*, you think, for that was the exact reason you had started to make your call. Carl Jung, the imminent Swiss psychiatrist, called these moments *synchronicities*, which he defined as "meaningful coincidences." There is enormous power behind these events, for they can open us up in a fresh new way. Synchronicity connects us to something to which we need to be connected. For example, the quote shared by the friends might contain a valuable piece of information that one or both of them had consciously or unconsciously been looking for. We must not simply be amazed at these moments; we must take them seriously and allow ourselves to be open to the wisdom given to us.

Coincidence is God's way of staying invisible.

—Albert Einstein

TEACHERS

Poor is the pupil who does not surpass his teacher.

—Leonardo da Vinci

Try to recall all the teachers you have had in your life, beginning in kindergarten. List them on paper. Then go through and mark the most significant ones. When you do this, ask yourself, if this person had not been in my life how would I be different? Many educators have shaped us and started us down paths we would not have taken on our own. In the Orient the term *guru* is used for a spiritual teacher. The word means "heavy." This implies that these special teachers were strongly rooted in principles and were gifted not only with wisdom but with loving spirits. It is wonderful to honor these wise ones in your life by remembering the contributions they made to the person you are today.

Teachers open the door, but you must enter by yourself.

—Chinese Proverb

TEARS

It is such a secret place, the land of tears.

—Antoine de Saint-Exupery

One of the hardest things we must do as a family member or as a good friend is watch tears flow down the cheeks of someone we hold dear. Even though we might be able to momentarily stop the flow of tears, they often remain inside. Some of us are more comfortable with tears than others, perhaps because we easily allow our own tears to fall and are more used to them. The greatest gift we can give a loved one is to be with them when they cry, accept their tears, and know that we cannot go where their personal pain is taking them. All we can do is be gently and quietly in their space and love them through the pain.

. . . suffering . . . no matter how multiplied . . . is always individual.

—Anne Morrow Lindbergh

TEETER-TOTTER

Have patience with all things, but chiefly have patience with yourself.

—St. Frances de Sales

How quickly our lives can be thrown out of balance. Just when we think we have everything in its proper place, a person or event throws their weight on our side of a teeter-totter and down we go. Often the sudden jar of being thrown so quickly off balance can be painful. Too many commitments, too many chores, and too many people in our lives who want and expect our time and attention probably bring on the imbalance. Many of these tasks and chores are self-imposed, and if we want to bring balance back into our lives we must simplify. This cannot be done in a day or even a week, but it is a task within our capabilities. No one likes to be on the down side of a teeter-totter, feeling stuck, heavy, out of control, and immobile. But as you start removing some of the unnecessary tasks and activities, the weight will slowly shift, and you will once again find balance that restores focus and harmony to your life.

The key to finding a happy balance in modern life is simplicity.

—Sogyal Rinpoche

TENACITY

Success is dependent on effort.

—Sophocles

It is a special experience to watch a determined person refuse to give up even when all the odds are against him or her. They are like a tiny dog hanging onto the end of a sock or shoe, and no matter how hard the master tries to get them to release the toy, the little thing absolutely refuses to give it up. One wonders if people are born with different tenacity quotients or if everyone has the same amount of inner strength and determination. There is a big difference between tenacity and stubbornness. Being stubborn is indicative that you want your way and may use cowardly means to get it. The tenacious person, however, demonstrates courage, and their end goal is often for the benefit of others. On a scale of one to ten, where would you place your tenacity level? Do you think you are more stubborn or more tenacious? Often we are more tenacious than we think. Try to remember the time when you were the most determined to gain a goal that benefited more than just your self-interest. If you possessed this trait at one time in your life, you can be sure it is still there and can be found within you once again.

Let me tell you the secret that has led to my goal. My strength is my tenacity.

—Louis Pasteur

THIS IS YOUR LIFE

The longer I live the more beautiful life becomes.
—Frank Lloyd Wright

When black-and-white television first came into our living rooms, one of the most popular programs was *This Is Your Life*. Every week the producers brought a celebrity onstage, made them comfortable on a sofa, and then unrolled their past. Coming from offstage, the guest would hear forgotten voices from the past: relatives, classmates, teachers, old roommates, and friends. The fun and excitement of the program came from watching the celebrity's face as he or she recognized the voice and then recalled the stories being told. The celebrity would gasp and scream, and the mystery person would be led onstage to receive hugs and kisses. If you could write your own episode of *This Is Your Life*, who would you like to be on your show? What stories would they tell about you? Can you remember the sound of their voices? When we recall these special moments and people, time stands still and it is as if nothing separates us from these treasured moments.

Now join hands and with your hands your hearts.
—William Shakespeare

TIME CAPSULE

Study the past, if you would divine the future.

—Confucius

In your mind create a time capsule for your life. What items would you include that encapsulate each of the decades you have lived? Into this canister place one book, five photographs, four small objects, a newspaper or magazine from any time in your life, a significant letter you have received or sent, and one other item of your choice. Now imagine an archaeologist digging up this time capsule 500 years from the date you bury it. What kind of story would this scientist piece together about your life? Would these objects accurately tell him about the history that surrounded you? To get a feel of how history has impacted your life, ask yourself these questions: What invention most changed my life? What artistic and literary creations were my biggest inspirations? What historical event most changed my life? What famous person most affected my thinking? We are all part and parcel of every event that came before us, and we are also individually a part of this grand puzzle that we call history.

Life can only be understood backwards, but it must be lived forward.

—Søren Kierkegaard

TOUCH

Hands that give also receive.

—Equadorian Proverb

It is wonderful to watch a newborn animal being licked by its mother into new life. Over and over the mother washes it and awakens it to the world. Touch is as essential to our existence as food and water. Our bodies yearn for it, and when we are deprived an overwhelming feeling of loneliness descends on us. Studies have shown that small children who are not touched simply do not flourish or grow up to be as healthy in mind and body as those who have been cuddled and hugged. The Touch Research Institute discovered that touch reduces stress hormones, alleviates depression, reduces pain, and positively alters the immune system. We have all been given a license to dispense this wonderful medicine, and we should take every opportunity to use it. The moment we reach out and touch someone, whether it is a big hug or a quick and gentle touch on the hand, we make a connection between two bodies and two hearts. How many people have you touched today?

I hate the giving of the hand unless the whole man accompanies it.

—Ralph Waldo Emerson

TOYS

You can discover more about a person in an hour of play than in a year of conversation.

—Plato

A trip to a large toy store is an eye-opening adventure: thousands upon thousands of brightly colored cellophane-wrapped boxes reach to the ceiling. People rush up and down the aisles with carts heaped with treasures; children follow clamoring for more toys to be added to the cartload. We are fortunate to live at a time when we have so many choices and resources. But does abundance bring more joy or fun? When we were children our choices at a toy store were limited. Our toy chests were never empty, but they were not as full as the closets and shelves of children today. We often had one doll for years and loved it so much that frequent visits to the doll hospital were required. The more we have, whether shoes or dolls, the more time we must spend in making decisions on which one to play with or which one to wear. We move from object to object, never being with one long enough to truly learn to treasure it. Less does equal more when it gives us the chance to deeply appreciate and love all the things that have been placed in our lives.

Familiar acts are beautiful through love.

—Percy Bysshe Shelley

THE TREE OF LIFE

*Separate reeds are weak and easily broken, but bound
together they are strong and hard to pull apart.*

—The Midrash

The Tree of Life is a symbol we find in the Bible, Mayan legends,
Scandinavian prophecies, the mystical Kabbalah, and shamanic cultures around the world. In some of these traditions the tree is a symbol
of a pact made between God and man. In shamanic cultures the Tree
of Life is the *Axis Mundi*, the center of all existence, and the shaman
uses it to climb to the upper world or follow its roots into the lower
world. In Taos Pueblo, in New Mexico, a tree that is cut in a sacred
manner is raised in the center of the plaza during the harvest festival of
San Geronimo. The members of the clown society attempt to climb to
the top where there are bags of food and freshly butchered meat. The
Celts of ancient Europe celebrated the coming of spring by erecting a
Maypole that was the center of the rites of this season. Today in many
homes we gather around a Christmas tree that becomes the center for
the family's celebration. All these trees are erected for slightly different
reasons, but they all share the purpose of creating a center around
which a family or a community can gather. Today our communities
and our families seem to lack an *Axis Mundi*, and we need to find
ways to create an inner core so all the members of the group can find
unity and balance within the circle. Do you have an *Axis Mundi*, a
center for your life and the life of your family? Where is it located? If
you do not have one, how could you create a heartfelt center?

*Sages speak of the immutable Tree of Life, with its tap
root above and its branches below.*

—Bhagavad Gita

TREE RINGS

A monk said, is there anything more miraculous than the wonders of nature? The master answered: Yes, your awareness of nature.

—Hui Hai

Have you ever tried to count the rings on a tree trunk? As your fingers creep across the cut surface, they often find it difficult to separate one ring from the next. The rings are the diaries of a tree's life. Each year a tree grows, it develops one ring on both its trunk and branches. The variations of the rings are caused by the many conditions that affect the tree: moisture, temperature, soil, and sunlight. When a tree is under stress, its rings show a great deal of variation; scientists call this "sensitivity." When a tree has had a season of stability and the rings are more regular, they are called "complacent." How similar our lives are to a tree's. Our growth depends on the things that surround us and how we respond to each one. Some years we know we are more sensitive and others more complacent. Imagine your life as a freshly cut tree trunk with fifty, seventy-five, or ninety rings circling inside it. Can you remember why the thirtieth ring looks broad and even, or why the fifty-fifth has ragged variations? We often see our life as a line we move along from the point of birth to death. It is also interesting to see it as a circle, with each ring embracing and defining the one that came before.

Yesterday is history. Tomorrow is mystery. And today? Today is a gift.

—Babafunde Olafunji

TREES

Did you once have a tree house? Were you a climber and swinger of trees? Did you sit under drooping canopies of limbs to hide from situations that were out of your control? Throughout our lives trees have been some of our best playmates and most supportive friends. When life becomes overwhelming, a walk through an orchard or a hike into a wood can lift our spirits and often bring solutions to problems that have been with us for a long time. It is not merely the exercise that helps our minds and bodies; it is being in the company of trees. When next you become bogged down with painful issues and anxieties that float aimlessly through your mind, make a date with a tree. It is not hard to understand their language. Just hold the trunk, a branch, or a leaf, and their wise support and love will flow into you.

TURTLE ISLAND

Holy Mother Earth, the trees and all nature are witnesses of your thoughts and deeds.

—Winnebago Saying

Native Americans honor the turtle because of the sacrifice one made many ages ago. Legend says there was a time when humans were in conflict and had forgotten the interconnection of all of life. The Creator was sad and disappointed, for she needed humans to bring forth her vision of the world. Because they would not change their ways she called the spirits to cover the land with water. Later, a spirit woman asked the Creator for a mate so she could bring forth new life for the world. She was granted her request, but the couple had no place to live and raise a family, for the land had disappeared. Soon a giant turtle came and told them that a muskrat would bring earth to cover his shell and they could build a dwelling there. To honor the turtle the first couple named their home Turtle Island. Many people today refer to our planet by this name. It is a title that shows a belief in the interconnections between humans and all the creatures that give us sustenance, protection, and delight.

I wonder if the ground has anything to say? I wonder if the ground is listening to what is said? The ground says, it is the Great Spirit that placed me here.

—Young Chief of the Cayuses

TWENTY-FOUR HOURS

Without a purpose nothing should be done.
—Marcus Aurelius

It is an interesting exercise to take one day and log how much time you spend on various activities: housework, sleeping, alone time, hobbies, watching TV, reading, exercising, writing letters, being with friends, surfing the Internet, etc. In order to see where your time really goes, make a pie graph and divide your various activities into different pieces of the pie. The size of the piece should reflect the amount of time spent in the activity. Now take a look at this picture of a typical day. Are you happy with the way you spend your twenty-four hours? Are your activities worthwhile and are they giving you satisfaction? What changes do you want to make? Create an ideal day with another pie graph. Could your ideal day become your every day?

Our life is frittered away by detail.
—Henry David Thoreau

VITALITY

To do nothing is sometimes a great remedy.

—Hippocrates

There is a difference between a person's energy and their vitality. Energy is what gets us through the day; vitality is the life force within us, the radiant power that helps us grow and transform. We see this vitality in a flower about to burst forth in bloom. Soon it will open up and its scent and beauty will flow into the world. It is easy to lose our vitality, for it takes more than healthy food and exercise to maintain it. It is sustained when we search inside ourselves for the source of our life and creativity. We know and feel when this vital force is leaking out, and we must immediately nourish it so it will continue to give us the energy to bloom.

Look within . . . the secret is inside you.

—Hui-Neng

VORTEX

The nature of infinity is this: That everything has its own vortex.

—William Blake

The word "vortex" comes from the Latin *vertere*, which means to twirl and swirl about. The dictionary describes a vortex as whirling fluid motion of energy that travels swiftly along an axis. A vortex can be made up of anything that flows: water, wind, electricity, or fire. We live in a world of vortices: hurricanes, tornadoes, whirlpools, and even the water spiraling down our drains. Vortices can move in different ways: some spiral out like our solar system; others contract like a whirlpool; and some are even ossified like the conch or snail shell. The spiral is a symbol found in all cultures and carries within it the meanings of growth, creativity, wisdom, and change. Our life situation and our affairs often resemble the spiraling of a vortex. We often feel trapped within its overwhelming, unceasing energy, but we can also move along its spiral, reaching new dimensions of growth and wisdom.

The human being always makes progress, but it is a progress of spirals.

—Madame de Stael

WALKING

Solvitur ambulando. "It is solved by walking."
—St. Augustine

"Take a problem for a walk" is always good advice. A walk does not have to be long or even brisk. Fresh air and movement are excellent medicines, for they give the brain and heart a needed break from any turmoil you might be feeling. The important thing is that you do not carry your problems into your walk, for if your mind races around the concerns your steps will quicken and the anxiety cannot be released. One way to distract our minds from a problem is to link our breathing to our steps. Thich Nhat Hanh, a Vietnamese Buddhist monk, suggests using a calming phrase like "With each step, a gentle wind blows." Another simple distraction is to name the beautiful and fascinating things you see and describe them in a few words: a brown pine cone dangling from a tree; two black squirrels playing hide and seek; a dandelion seedhead all puffed out and ready to blow away. Let what you observe draw you into the moment that you have wisely given yourself. When you return from your walk your problems will not have vanished, but you will have gained some balance and focus so you can handle them with a fresh new perspective. If this doesn't happen, go out and walk again.

> *The mind can go in a thousand directions.*
> *But on this beautiful path, I walk in peace.*
> *With each step, a gentle wind blows.*
> *With each step, a flower blossoms.*
>
> —Thich Nhat Hanh

WALLS

People are lonely because they build walls instead of bridges.

—Joseph F. Newton

There have been many great walls constructed throughout history: the Great Wall of China, the Walls of Jericho, Hadrian's Wall, and the protective walls of medieval castles. All were built to keep a group secure and safe from their enemies. This method of protection worked for thousands of years, and then man invented weapons that made these walls obsolete. In our lives we also build walls to keep people out and to protect ourselves from conflict and difficult situations. These walls are not made of bricks and stones but are constructed of invisible material. We build them with thoughts like, "This person does not look like me or act like me, so I will exclude them from my life." When we build walls to protect us from other people or events, we risk losing opportunities and experiences that will challenge us and help us grow. When we find ourselves constructing walls, it would be good to remember a line from the poet Robert Frost, "Before I built a wall I'd ask to know what I was walling in or walling out."

With the help of God, I shall leap over the wall.

—Book of Common Prayer

WAR

Life only demands from you the strength that you possess.
—Dag Hammarskjöld

We are all victims of war, but children always suffer the most. We cry when we see war photos and videos that show tiny refugees fleeing their homes to be placed in leaky tents in a camp far away from their beloved towns and villages. We mourn over the children with swollen bellies and become indignant that a war has robbed them of food. And we shed tears for the babies crying over the bodies of someone they loved and who cared for them. Perhaps if we engraved these images on our hearts and our minds, we would not allow wars to occur. In every nation of the world children are the ones we love the most, and yet we are willing to allow them to suffer unbearable pain and loss. Two million children have died in dozens of wars in the past decade. As long as both sides in a war allow children to be the victims, there can never be a victor. Politicians declare wars and we often feel powerless over their decisions, but each of us has a voice and we can cry out to insist that the world listen to the cries of the children.

Sin by silence when they could protest makes cowards out of men.

—Abraham Lincoln

WATER

The best, like water, benefit all and do not compete.

—Lao Tzu

According to the ancient Greek philosopher Thales, everything is composed of water. Maybe that is why our body resonates when we walk on a beach or sit by a babbling brook. For thousands of years people have purified their bodies and souls with water. The sacrament of baptism washes Christians of their sins, the ancient Greeks stopped at sacred springs to wash before they entered their holy sites, and the Hindus believe the sacred Ganges River has the power and energy to purify them. Water assures us of our existence, and yet we may turn on our household taps ten times a day to get a glass of water and not think about its source or its necessity for our daily living. The treated water we hold in our hands was once rain, sleet, hail, or snow. We drink water that has dwelled in the depths of the earth for thousands of years. When you drink your next glass of water, think about its source and thank each drop for its life-sustaining gift.

This is it! This is it! Look at it! Isn't it bubbling?

—Joseph Campbell

WEB

"What's miraculous about a spider's web?" said Mrs.
Arabe. "I don't see why you're saying a web is a miracle;
it's just a web." "Ever try to spin one?" asked Mr. Darian.

—E.B. White

Many people are frightened of spiders because of their many jointed
legs and their fast and secretive movements. We all, however, stand in
awe and wonder when we see one of their creations on a summer
morning dripping with silvery dewdrops. We gasp at the marvel of a
spider's overnight creation. Our scientific knowledge and technological skills have allowed us to create the World Wide Web and put
rockets into space, but we are incapable of constructing a weaving
with the tiniest filaments that flow from the inner core of our bodies.
When we gaze at a spider's web we can remember that we are not separate entities but are all interconnected: you to me, both of us to earth,
earth to rocks, rocks to mountains, mountains to trees, and on and on
in a never-ending chain within a glorious web.

What is life? It is a flash of a firefly in the night . . . the
breath of a buffalo in the winter time . . . a little shadow
which runs across the grass and loses itself in the sunset.

—Crowfoot (1821)

WISDOM

When you understand, you cannot help but love.

—Thich Nhat Hanh

There is a big difference between one who possesses knowledge and one who possesses wisdom. Wisdom is a deep spiritual knowing of what path to walk. It is a strong desire to see the unity of all life. It is the ability to move slowly. It is the capacity to see all life as interconnecting circles. Wisdom comes when one is patient with oneself and with others. The result is a life lived with loving compassion.

Do not seek to follow in the footsteps of the wise. Seek what they sought.

—Basho

WITCH HUNTS

Rely on your wisdom mind, not on your ordinary judgmental mind.

—The Buddha

When we think of the medieval witch hunts of history we think of the tortured, innocent women accused of casting spells and flying through the night sky on broomsticks. We also recall the Salem trials where innocent men and women were executed because they were falsely accused by teenage girls who were victims of seventeenth-century peer pressure. Today we feel that we are much too sophisticated to point a finger at someone and cry, "Witch!" Yet exaggerated and false accusations take place on a daily basis. Today the sentence will not be to burn the person at the stake, but it might mean ostracism from a group. We easily criticize our ancestors for their witch hunts, and yet we too give in to prejudice and intolerance.

A great many people think they are thinking when they are rearranging their prejudices.

—Edward R. Murrow

WHO'S WHO

I hope I never get too old to listen to the advice of a wise person.

—Socrates

As the world inched toward the millennium, historians around the world were busy creating lists of the most influential people of the last 1,000 years. There was much debate about whether Isaac Newton, Napoleon, Martin Luther King Jr., Albert Einstein, or Winston Churchill should be on the list. Everyone had their favorite. In our personal lives, significant individuals have influenced us and even changed our course. Make your own "Who's Who" list of the most significant people in your life. Start with a list of ten and then rank them if you can. Names on your list will include family members, friends, and mentors as well as famous people. When your list is complete you will have before you the people who prodded, inspired, and led you to where you are today.

The doors of wisdom are never shut.

—Benjamin Franklin

WONDERS OF THE WORLD

He who wonders discovers that this in itself is wonder.
—M. C. Escher

Can you name the Seven Wonders of the Ancient World?* As children we were curious about the images of these ancient sites that had such enchanting names: the Hanging Gardens of Babylon, the Mausoleum of Halicarnassus, the Colossus of Rhodes. How much easier it is today for us to create and construct such wonders. No longer do men and women have to carry tons of brick and stone on their backs to create awe-inspiring structures. What a culture considers "a wonder" tells a great deal about their values and lifestyles. For example, the pyramids were dedicated to god-kings, and the Hanging Gardens were for the enjoyment of an absolute monarch. Today we value far different things: technology, wealth, and fame. What do you think the Seven Wonders of the twenty-first century will be? What you envision tells you the direction in which you think your society is moving. Are you comfortable with what you foresee as the future goals and values of your culture?

Seven Wonders of the Ancient World: the Pyramids, the Lighthouse of Alexandria, the Hanging Gardens of Babylon, the Temple of Artemis, the Statue of Zeus, the Mausoleum at Halicarnassus, the Colossus of Rhodes

WORDS

The words that enlighten the soul are more precious than jewels.

—Hazrat Inayat Khan

Here is a difficult assignment: try to go one day without reading anything—no newspapers, magazines, letters, cereal boxes, or books. Most of us could not make it through twenty-four hours; in fact, we might not be able to make it through four. We probably would miss our reading more than TV, radio, or even meals, for words connect us to our friends and to our world. C. S. Lewis wrote, "We read to know that we are not alone." We have many motives for reading: to relax, to fall asleep, to prevent boredom, and to escape events that are transpiring in our lives. Depriving ourselves of our reading material often makes our motives clear. What you might want to do during this period of abstinence is write instead of read. But, of course, do not read what you write until the next day.

By words the mind is winged.

—Aristophanes

WRINKLES

Those who the gods love grow young.

—Oscar Wilde

Most of us can remember the exact moment when we looked in the mirror and saw our first gray hair or the first noticeable wrinkle on our face. We were still young, perhaps only in our twenties. Year by year our faces and bodies change at such a slow pace that we often don't perceive what is taking place until we catch a glimpse of ourselves in the reflection of a window and wonder who that person might be. It takes a certain amount of courage to face these changes. We are told that we should be proud of our wrinkles, for we have earned each one. That is true, but it is still hard when we live in a youth-oriented culture to love the physical changes that take place. We could hide some of our physical changes and the world might be fooled, but would we really want to? When we worry about these changes, it is important to remember all the friends, relatives, and acquaintances who died prematurely and who did not have a chance to see and feel themselves maturing and aging. Every stage of life is unique, and we will miss this special stage if we do not accept the beauty of our changing faces and bodies.

> *Generally by the time you are Real, most of your hair has been loved off and your eyes drop out and you get loose in the joints and shabby. But these things don't matter at all because once you are Real you can't be ugly, except to people who don't understand.*
>
> —Margery Wiliams, *The Velveteen Rabbit*

BIBLIOGRAPHY

Ackerman, Diane. *A Natural History of the Senses*. New York: Harper and Row, 1994.

Artess, Lauren. *Walking the Sacred Path: Rediscovering the Labyrinth as a Sacred Tool*. New York: Riverhead Books, 1995.

Baker, Jeremy. *Tolstoy's Bicycle*. New York: St. Martin's Press, 1982.

Bartlett, John. *Familiar Quotations*. 14th edition. Boston: Little, Brown and Company, 1968.

Beecher, Henry Ward. *Selections from the Works of Henry Ward Beecher*. Boston: Caldwell, 1902.

Bender, Sue. *Everyday Sacred*. San Francisco: HarperSanFrancisco, 1995.

———. *Plain and Simple: A Women's Journey to Amish Country*. San Francisco: Harper and Row, 1989.

Blake, William. *The Marriage of Heaven and Hell*. New York: E. P. Dutton and Co., 1927.

———. *Songs of Innocence and Songs of Experience*. Princeton: William Blake Trust/Princeton University Press, 1991.

Bohm, David. *Wholeness and the Implicate Order*. London: Routledge and Kegan, 1980.

Book of Songs. Mount Vernon NY: Peter Pauper Press.

Browning, Robert. *Letters and Poetry*. New York: Doubleday, 1970.

Buber, Martin. *I and Thou*. New York: Touchstone, 1966.

Burgess, Gelett. *Purple Cow and Other Nonsense*. New York: Dover, 1961.

Carroll, Lewis. *Through the Looking Glass*. New York: Doubleday, 1982.

Cather, Willa. *My Antonia*. Boston: Houghton Mifflin, 1954.

Chaucer, Geoffrey. *The Canterbury Tales*. New York: Modern Library, 1994.

Campbell, Joseph, and Bill Moyers. *The Power of Myth*. New York: Doubleday, 1988.

Chesterton, G. K. *Chesterton's Stories, Essays and Poems*. Everyman's Library: Essays & Belles, letters, no. 913. London: J. M. Dent & Sons, 1935.

———. *Tremendous Trifles*. New York: Dodd, Mead and Co., 1922.

Cloud of Unknowing. New York: Paulist Press, 1981.

Collison, Robert, and Mary Collison, ed. *Dictionary of Foreign Quotations*. New York: Facts on File, 1980.

Columbia Book of Quotations. New York: Columbia University Press, 1993.

Dalai Lama. *The Dalai Lama's Book of Wisdom*. New York: Thorson, 2000.

———. *The Essential Teachings: His Holiness of Dalai Lama*. Berkeley: North Atlantic Press, 1995.

———. *The Path of Tranquillity*. New York: Viking, 1999.

Dossey, Larry. *Space, Time and Medicine*. Boston: New Science Library, 1985.

Easwaran Eknath. *Conquest of the Mind*. Petaluma CA: Nilgiri Press, 1988.

———. *Your Life Is Your Message*. New York: Hyperion, 1992.

———. *Words to Live By*. Petaluma CA: Nilgiri Press, 1996.

Einstein, Albert. *Ideas and Opinions*. New York: Crown Publisher, 1954.

———. *The Quotable Einstein*. Collected and edited by Alice Calaprice. Princeton: Princeton University Press, 1996.

———. *The World As I See It*. New York: Carol Publishing Group, 1999.

Emerson, Ralph Waldo. *The Complete Writings of Ralph Waldo Emerson*. New York: Wm. H. Wise and Co., 1929.

Fischer, Louis, ed. *The Essential Gandhi: An Anthology His Life, Work and Ideas*. New York: Vintage Books, 1962.

Frank, Anne. *Diary of a Young Girl*. New York: Modern Library, 1952.

Frankl, Viktor. *Man's Search for Meaning*. Boston: Beacon Press, 1992.

Frost, Robert. *Robert Frost's Poems*. New York: The Pocket Library, 1956.

Gandhi, Mohandes K. *All Men are Brothers: The Life and Thoughts of Mahatma Gandhi As Told In His Words*. Edited by Krishna Kripalani. Paris: Unesco Publications, 1960.

———. *An Autobiography: The Story of My Experiments With Truth*. Boston: Beacon Hill, 1957.

Gibran, Kahlil. *A Treasury of Kalhil Gibran*. Edited by Martin L. Wolf. New York: The Citadel Press, 1954.

———. *The Prophet*. New York: Alfred A. Knopf, 1966.

Goethe, Johann Wolfgang von. *The Permanent Goethe*. New York: Dial Press, 1948.

Hallie, Phillip. *Lest Innocent Blood Be Shed*. New York: Harper Torchbooks, 1979.

Hammarskjöld, Dag. *Markings*. New York: Knopf, 1964.

Holmes, Oliver Wendell. *"Chambered Nautilus." Complete Poetical Works of Oliver Wendell Holmes*. New York: Houghton, 1910.

Holy Bible, King James Version. New York: The World Publishing Company.

Jade Flute: Chinese Poems in Prose. Mount Vernon NY: Pauper Press, 1960.

James, William. *Writings 1842–1910*. New York: Literary Classics ofthe United States, 1987.

Keating, Thomas. *Active Meditations for Contemplative Prayer*. New York: Continuum, 1997.

———. *Invitation to Love*. New York: Continuum, 1999.

———. *Open Mind, Open Heart*. New York: Continuum, 1997.

Keller, Helen. *The Story of My Life*. New York: Doubleday, Page and Company, 1903.

Kierkegaard, Søren. *A Kierkegaard Anthology*. Edited by Robert Bretall. New York: Modern Library, 1959.

Lao Tze. *Tao Te Ching*. Translated by John C. H. Wu. Boston: Shambhala, 1989.

Lin, Yutang. *The Importance of Living*. New York: W. Morrow, 1996.

Lindbergh, Anne Morrow. *Gift From the Sea*. New York: Pantheon Books, 1977.

———. *War Within and Without: Diaries and Letters of Anne Morrow Lindbergh 1935–1955*. San Diego: Harcourt Brace, 1995.

MacMillan Pubishing Company. *Macmillan Dictionary of Quotations*. New York: Macmillan, 1989.

Marcus Aurelius. *Meditations*. Translated by George Long. Buffalo NY: Prometheus Books, 1991.

Marke, Julius J., ed. *Holmes Reader*. New York: Oceana Publications, 1955.

McLuhan, T. C., ed. *Touch the Earth*. New York: Promontory Press, 1971.

Meister Eckhart. *From Whom God Hides Nothing*. Boston: Shambhala Publications, 1996.

Merton, Thomas. *New Seeds of Contemplation*. New York: New Directions Books, 1961.

———. *A Search for Solitude: Pursuing the Monk's True Life*. San Francisco: HarperSanFranciso, 1996.

Metzger, Deena. *Writing For Your Life*. San Francisco: HarperSanFrancisco, 1992.

Mother Teresa. *No Greater Love.* Novato CA: New World Library, 1997.

———. *In the Heart of the World: Thoughts, Stories and Prayers.* Novato CA: New World Library, 1997.

———. *In My Own Words.* Thorndike ME: G. K. Hall, 1996.

Moulthrop, Glenna Hammer, compiler. *Living In Love: A Compilation of Mother Teresa's Teaching on Love.* Nashville: Towle House Publishing Co., 2000.

Murphy Edward E., ed. *The Crown Treasure of Relevant Quotations.* New York: Crown Publishers, Inc., 1978.

Neihardt, John. *Black Elk Speaks.* Lincoln: University of Nebraska Press, 1961.

Nietzche, Fredrich. *The Portable Nietzche.* New York: Penguin Books, 1976.

One Hundred Best Poems for Girls and Boys. Edited by Marjorie Barrows. Racine WI: Whitman Publishing Company, 1930.

Osbon, Diana, ed. *The Joseph Campbell Reader.* New York: HarperCollins, 1991.

Pennington, Basil M. *Mary Today.* New York: Doubleday & Sons, 1987.

Roosevelt, Eleanor. *On My Own.* New York: Harper, 1958.

———. *This Is My Story.* New York: Harper and Brothers, 1937.

———. *What I Hope to Leave Behind: The Essential Essays of Eleanor Roosevelt.* Edited by Allida M Black. Brooklyn: Carlson Publishers, 1995.

Rumi. *Look! This Is Love: Poems by Rumi.* Translated by Ingrid Schaar. Boston: Shambhala Publications, 1996.

Saint-Exupéry, Antoine de. *The Little Prince.* New York: Harcourt-Brace, 1943.

———. *Wind, Sand, and Stars.* New York: Harbrace, 1939.

Safranshy, Sy, ed. *Sunbeams: A Book of Quotations.* Berkeley CA: North Atlantic Press, 1990.

Schweitzer, Albert. *Out of My Life and Thought: An Autobiography.* New York: H. Hold, 1949

Scott, Paul. *The Day of the Scorpion.* Chicago: University of Chicago Press, 1998.

Settet, Trudy, comp. *Wisdom of Gandhi.* New York: Philosophical Library, 1967.

Shakespeare, William. *Complete Works.* New York: Gramercy Books, 1975.

Shaw, Bernard. *Saint Joan.* New York: Penguin Books, 1988.

Shelley, Percy Bysshe. *Shelley Poetical Works.* Edited by Thomas Hitchinson. London: Oxford University Press, 1968.

Sogyal Rinpoche. *Glimpse After Glimpse.* San Francisco, HarperSanFrancisco, 1995.

Steindl-Rast, David. *Gratefulness the Heart of Prayer.* New York: Paulist Press, 1984.

———. *A Listening Heart: The Art of Contemplation.* New York: Crossroad, 1988.

Sutton, Joseph, ed. *Words of Wellness.* Carson CA: Hay House, Inc., 1991.

Suzuki Roshi. *Zen Mind, Beginner's Mind.* Edited by Trudy Dixon. New York: Witherhill. 1999.

Thomas à Kempis. *Imitation of Christ.* Notre Dame IN: Ave Maria Press, 1989.

Thoreau, Henry David. *Journal of Henry David Thoreau.* Edited by Bradford Torry and Francis H. Allen. Boston: Houghton Mifflin, 1949.

———. *Walden and Other Writings.* Edited by Brooks Atkinson, no. 155. New York: Modern Library, 1965.

Thich Nhat Hanh. *Breathe! You Are Alive.* Berkeley CA: Parallax Press, 1996.

———. *A Guide to Walking Meditation.* Berkeley CA: Parallax Press, 1985.

———. *Peace in Every Step: The Path of Mindfulness in Everyday Life.* New York: Bantam Books, 1992.

———. *Present Moment, Wonderful Moment.* Berkeley CA: Parallax Press, 1990.

Tolstoy, Leo. *Wisdom of Humankind.* Translated by Guy de Mallac. Ada MI: CoNexus Press, 1999.

Tulku Thondup and Daniel Goldman. *The Healing Power of the Mind: Meditation Exercises for Health.* Boston: Shambhala Publications, 1996.

White, E. B. *Charlotte's Web.* New York: Harper/Econ/Perma, 1980.

Whitman, Walt. *Complete Poetry and Collected Prose.* New York: Viking Press, 1982.

———. *Leaves of Grass.* New York: Doubleday Doran and Co., Inc., 1940.

Wilde, Oscar. *Complete Works of Oscar Wilde.* London: Collins, 1966.

Williams, Margery. *The Velveteen Rabbit.* New York: Knopf, 1985.

Wit and Wisdom of Albert Schweitzer. Ed. Charles R. Roy. Boston: Beacon Press, 1949.

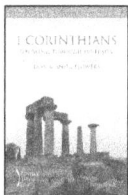

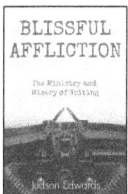

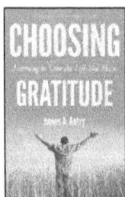

Choosing Gratitude
Learning to Love the Life You Have

James A. Autry

Autry reminds us that gratitude is a choice, a spiritual—not social—process. He suggests that if we cultivate gratitude as a way of being, we may not change the world and its ills, but we can change our response to the world. If we fill our lives with moments of gratitude, we will indeed love the life we have.   978-1-57312-614-4 144 pages/pb **$15.00**

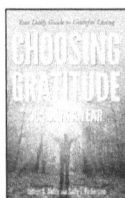

Choosing Gratitude 365 Days a Year
Your Daily Guide to Grateful Living

James A. Autry and Sally J. Pederson

Filled with quotes, poems, and the inspired voices of both Pederson and Autry, in a society consumed by fears of not having "enough"—money, possessions, security, and so on—this book suggests that if we cultivate gratitude as a way of being, we may not change the world and its ills, but we can change our response to the world.   978-1-57312-689-2 210 pages/pb **$18.00**

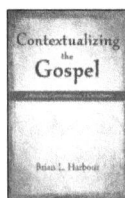

Contextualizing the Gospel
A Homiletic Commentary on 1 Corinthians

Brian L. Harbour

Harbour examines every part of Paul's letter, providing a rich resource for those who want to struggle with the difficult texts as well as the simple texts, who want to know how God's word—all of it—intersects with their lives today.   978-1-57312-589-5 240 pages/pb **$19.00**

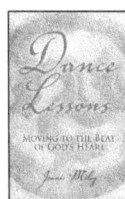

Dance Lessons
Moving to the Beat of God's Heart

Jeanie Miley

Miley shares her joys and struggles a she learns to "dance" with the Spirit of the Living God.   978-1-57312-622-9 240 pages/pb **$19.00**

A Divine Duet
Ministry and Motherhood

Alicia Davis Porterfield, ed.

Each essay in this inspiring collection is as different as the mother-minister who wrote it, from theologians to chaplains, inner-city ministers to rural-poverty ministers, youth pastors to preachers, mothers who have adopted, birthed, and done both.

978-1-57312-676-2 146 pages/pb **$16.00**

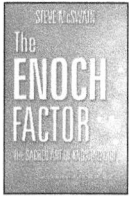

The Enoch Factor
The Sacred Art of Knowing God

Steve McSwain

The Enoch Factor is a persuasive argument for a more enlightened
religious dialogue in America, one that affirms the goals of all
religions—guiding followers in self-awareness, finding serenity
and happiness, and discovering what the author describes as "the sacred art of
knowing God." 978-1-57312-556-7 256 pages/pb **$21.00**

Ethics as if Jesus Mattered
Essays in Honor of Glen H. Stassen

Rick Axtell, Michelle Tooley, Michael L. Westmoreland-White, eds.

Ethics as if Jesus Mattered will introduce Stassen's work to a new
generation, advance dialogue and debate in Christian ethics, and
inspire more faithful discipleship just as it honors one whom the
contributors consider a mentor. 978-1-57312-695-3 234 pages/pb **$18.00**

Healing Our Hurts
Coping with Difficult Emotions

Daniel Bagby

In *Healing Our Hurts*, Daniel Bagby identifies and explains all the
dynamics at play in these complex emotions. Offering practical
biblical insights to these feelings, he interprets faith-based responses
to separate overly religious piety from true, natural human emotion. This book
helps us learn how to deal with life's difficult emotions in a redemptive and
responsible way. 978-1-57312-613-7 144 pages/pb **$15.00**

Help! I Teach Youth Sunday School

Brian Foreman, Bo Prosser, and David Woody

Real-life stories are mingled with information on Youth and their
culture, common myths about Sunday School, a new way of preparing the Sunday school lesson, creative teaching ideas, ways to think
about growing a class, and how to reach out for new members and
reach in to old members. 1-57312-427-3 128 pages/pb **$14.0**

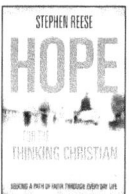

Hope for the Thinking Christian
Seeking a Path of Faith through Everyday Life

Stephen Reese

Readers who want to confront their faith more directly, to think it
through and be open to God in an individual, authentic, spiritual
encounter will find a resonant voice in Stephen Reese.

978-1-57312-553-6 160 pages/pb **$16.00**

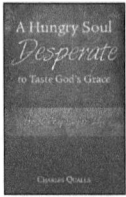

A Hungry Soul Desperate to Taste God's Grace
Honest Prayers for Life

Charles Qualls

Part of how we *see* God is determined by how we *listen* to God. There is so much noise and movement in the world that competes with images of God. This noise would drown out God's beckoning voice and distract us. Charles Qualls's newest book offers readers prayers for that journey toward the meaning and mystery of God. *978-1-57312-648-9 152 pages/pb* **$14.00**

James M. Dunn and Soul Freedom
Aaron Douglas Weaver

James Milton Dunn, over the last fifty years, has been the most aggressive Baptist proponent for religious liberty in the United States. Soul freedom—voluntary, uncoerced faith and an unfettered individual conscience before God—is the basis of his understanding of church-state separation and the historic Baptist basis of religious liberty. *978-1-57312-590-1 224 pages/pb* **$18.00**

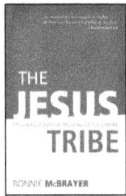

The Jesus Tribe
Following Christ in the Land of the Empire

Ronnie McBrayer

The Jesus Tribe fleshes out the implications, possibilities, contradictions, and complexities of what it means to live within the Jesus Tribe and in the shadow of the American Empire.

978-1-57312-592-5 208 pages/pb **$17.00**

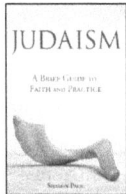

Judaism
A Brief Guide to Faith and Practice

Sharon Pace

Sharon Pace's newest book is a sensitive and comprehensive introduction to Judaism. What is it like to be born into the Jewish community? How does belief in the One God and a universal morality shape the way in which Jews see the world? How does one find meaning in life and the courage to endure suffering? How does one mark joy and forge community ties? *978-1-57312-644-1 144 pages/pb* **$16.00**

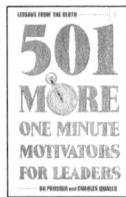

Lessons from the Cloth 2
501 More One Minute Motivators for Leaders

Bo Prosser and Charles Qualls

As the force that drives organizations to accomplishment, leadership is at a crucial point in churches, corporations, families, and almost every arena of life. In this follow-up to their first volume, Prosser and Qualls will inspire you to keep growing in your leadership career.

978-1-57312-665-6 152 pages/pb **$11.00**

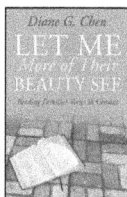

Let Me More of Their Beauty See
Reading Familiar Verses in Context
Diane G. Chen

Let Me More of Their Beauty See offers eight examples of how attention to the historical and literary settings can safeguard against taking a text out of context, bring out its transforming power in greater dimension, and help us apply Scripture appropriately in our daily lives.

978-1-57312-564-2 160 pages/pb **$17.00**

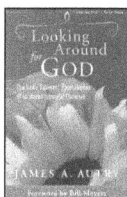

Looking Around for God
The Strangely Reverent Observations of an Unconventional Christian
James A. Autry

Looking Around for God, Autry's tenth book, is in many ways his most personal. In it he considers his unique life of faith and belief in God. Autry is a former Fortune 500 executive, author, poet, and consultant whose work has had a significant influence on leadership thinking.

978-157312-484-3 144 pages/pb **$16.00**

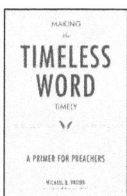

Making the Timeless Word Timely
A Primer for Preachers
Michael B. Brown

Michael Brown writes, "There is a simple formula for sermon preparation that creates messages that apply and engage whether your parish is rural or urban, young or old, rich or poor, five thousand members or fifty." The other part of the task, of course, involves being creative and insightful enough to know how to take the general formula for sermon preparation and make it particular in its impact on a specific congregation. Brown guides the reader through the formula and the skills to employ it with excellence and integrity.

978-1-57312-578-9 160 pages/pb **$16.00**

Meeting Jesus Today
For the Cautious, the Curious, and the Committed
Jeanie Miley

Meeting Jesus Today, ideal for both individual study and small groups, is intended to be used as a workbook. It is designed to move readers from studying the Scriptures and ideas within the chapters to recording their journey with the Living Christ.

978-1-57312-677-9 320 pages/pb **$19.00**

The Ministry Life
101 Tips for New Ministers
John Killinger

Sharing years of wisdom from more than fifty years in ministry and teaching, *The Ministry Life: 101 Tips for New Ministers* by John Killinger is filled with practical advice and wisdom for a minister's day-to-day tasks as well as advice on intellectual and spiritual habits to keep ministers of any age healthy and fulfilled. *978-1-57312-662-5 244 pages/pb* **$19.00**

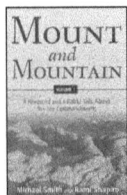

Mount and Mountain
Vol. 1: A Reverend and a Rabbi Talk About the Ten Commandments
Rami Shapiro and Michael Smith

Mount and Mountain represents the first half of an interfaith dialogue—a dialogue that neither preaches nor placates but challenges its participants to work both singly and together in the task of reinterpreting sacred texts. Mike and Rami discuss the nature of divinity, the power of faith, the beauty of myth and story, the necessity of doubt, the achievements, failings, and future of religion, and, above all, the struggle to live ethically and in harmony with the way of God. *978-1-57312-612-0 144 pages/pb* **$15.00**

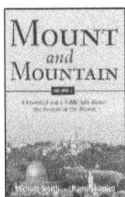

Mount and Mountain
Vol. 2: A Reverend and a Rabbi Talk About the Sermon on the Mount
Rami Shapiro and Michael Smith

This book, focused on the Sermon on the Mount, represents the second half of Mike and Rami's dialogue. In it, Mike and Rami explore the text of Jesus' sermon cooperatively, contributing perspectives drawn from their lives and religious traditions and seeking moments of illumination. *978-1-57312-654-0 254 pages/pb* **$19.00**

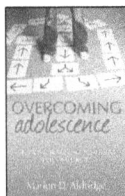

Overcoming Adolescence
Growing Beyond Childhood into Maturity
Marion D. Aldridge

In *Overcoming Adolescence*, Marion D. Aldridge poses questions for adults of all ages to consider. His challenge to readers is one he has personally worked to confront: to grow up *all the way*—mentally, physically, academically, socially, emotionally, and spiritually. The key involves not only knowing how to work through the process but also how to recognize what may be contributing to our perpetual adolescence.

978-1-57312-577-2 156 pages/pb **$17.00**

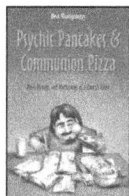

Psychic Pancakes & Communion Pizza
More Musings and Mutterings of a Church Misfit
Bert Montgomery

Psychic Pancakes & Communion Pizza is Bert Montgomery's highly anticipated follow-up to *Elvis, Willie, Jesus & Me* and contains further reflections on music, film, culture, life, and finding Jesus in the midst of it all.   *978-1-57312-578-9 160 pages/pb* **$16.00**

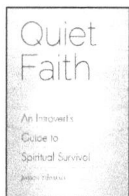

Quiet Faith
An Introvert's Guide to Spiritual Survival
Judson Edwards

In eight finely crafted chapters, Edwards looks at key issues like evangelism, interpreting the Bible, dealing with doubt, and surviving the church from the perspective of a confirmed, but sometimes reluctant, introvert. In the process, he offers some provocative insights that introverts will find helpful and reassuring.   *978-1-57312-681-6 144 pages/pb* **$15.00**

Reading Ezekiel (Reading the Old Testament series)
A Literary and Theological Commentary
Marvin A. Sweeney

The book of Ezekiel points to the return of YHWH to the holy temple at the center of a reconstituted Israel and creation at large. As such, the book of Ezekiel portrays the purging of Jerusalem, the Temple, and the people, to reconstitute them as part of a new creation at the conclusion of the book. With Jerusalem, the Temple, and the people so purged, YHWH stands once again in the holy center of the created world.

978-1-57312-658-8 264 pages/pb **$22.00**

Reading Hosea–Micah
(Reading the Old Testament series)
A Literary and Theological Commentary
Terence E. Fretheim

Terence E. Fretheim explores themes of indictment, judgment, and salvation in Hosea–Micah. The indictment against the people of God especially involves issues of idolatry, as well as abuse of the poor and needy. The effects of such behaviors are often horrendous in their severity. While God is often the subject of such judgments, the consequences, like fruit, grow out of the deed itself.   *978-1-57312-687-8 224 pages/pb* **$22.00**

Reading Samuel (Reading the Old Testament series)
A Literary and Theological Commentary
Johanna W. H. van Wijk-Bos

Interpreted masterfully by preeminent Old Testament scholar Johanna W. H. van Wijk-Bos, the story of Samuel touches on a vast array of subjects that make up the rich fabric of human life. The reader gains an inside look at leadership, royal intrigue, military campaigns, occult practices, and the significance of religious objects of veneration.

978-1-57312-607-6 272 pages/pb **$22.00**

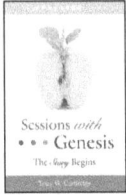

Sessions with Genesis (Session Bible Studies series)
The Story Begins
Tony W. Cartledge

Immersing us in the book of Genesis, Tony W. Cartledge examines both its major stories and the smaller cycles of hope and failure, of promise and judgment. Genesis introduces these themes of divine faithfulness and human failure in unmistakable terms, tracing Israel's beginning to the creation of the world and professing a belief that Israel's particular history had universal significance.

978-1-57312-636-6 144 pages/pb **$14.00**

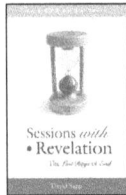

Sessions with Revelation (Session Bible Studies series)
The Final Days of Evil
David Sapp

David Sapp's careful guide through Revelation demonstrates that it is a letter of hope for believers; it is less about the last days of history than it is about the last days of evil. Without eliminating its mystery, Sapp unlocks Revelation's central truths so that its relevance becomes clear.

978-1-57312-706-6 166 pages/pb **$14.00**

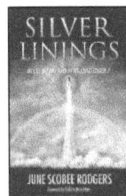

Silver Linings
My Life Before and After *Challenger 7*
June Scobee Rodgers

We know the public story of *Challenger 7*'s tragic destruction. That day, June's life took a new direction that ultimately led to the creation of the Challenger Center and to new life and new love. Her story of Christian faith and triumph over adversity will inspire readers of every age.

978-1-57312-570-3 352 pages/hc **$28.00**

978-1-57312-694-6 352 pages/pb **$18.00**

To order call **1-800-747-3016** or visit **www.helwys.com**

Spacious
Exploring Faith and Place

Holly Sprink

Exploring where we are and why that matters to God is an ongoing process. If we are present and attentive, God creatively and continuously widens our view of the world.   *978-1-57312-649-6 156 pages/pb* **$16.00**

The Teaching Church
Congregation as Mentor

Christopher M. Hamlin / Sarah Jackson Shelton

Collected in *The Teaching Church: Congregation as Mentor* are the stories of the pastors who shared how congregations have shaped, nurtured, and, sometimes, broken their resolve to be faithful servants of God.   *978-1-57312-682-3 112 pages/pb* **$13.00**

A Time to Laugh
Humor in the Bible

Mark E. Biddle

An extension of his well-loved seminary course on humor in the Bible, *A Time to Laugh* draws on Mark E. Biddle's command of Hebrew language and cultural subtleties to explore the ways humor was intentionally incorporated into Scripture. With characteristic liveliness, Biddle guides the reader through the stories of six biblical characters who did rather unexpected things.   *978-1-57312-683-0 164 pages/pb* **$14.00**

This Is What a Preacher Looks Like
Sermons by Baptist Women in Ministry

Pamela Durso, ed.

In this collection of sermons by thirty-six Baptist women, their voices are soft and loud, prophetic and pastoral, humorous and sincere. They are African American, Asian, Latina, and Caucasian. They are sisters, wives, mothers, grandmothers, aunts, and friends.

978-1-57312-554-3 144 pages/pb **$18.00**

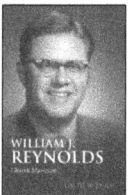

William J. Reynolds
Church Musician

David W. Music

William J. Reynolds is renowned among Baptist musicians, music ministers, song leaders, and hymnody students. In eminently readable style, David W. Music's comprehensive biography describes Reynolds's family and educational background, his career as a minister of music, denominational leader, and seminary professor.   *978-1-57312-690-8 358 pages/pb* **$23.00**

www.ingramcontent.com/pod-product-compliance
Lightning Source LLC
Chambersburg PA
CBHW051420090426
42737CB00014B/2754